the art of COMPREHENSION

the art of COMPREHENSION

Exploring Visual Texts to Foster Comprehension, Conversation, and Confidence

TREVOR ANDREW BRYAN

www.stenhouse.com

Credits
Figures I.1 and 2.1: Images courtesy of the Princeton University Art Museum.
Illustrations in Appendix B: Copyright © 2019 Kyle Stevenson.

Library of Congress Cataloging-in-Publication Data
Names: Bryan, Trevor Andrew, 1975- author.
Title: Art of comprehension : exploring visual texts to foster comprehension, conversation, and confidence / Trevor Andrew Bryan.
Description: Portsmouth, New Hampshire : Stenhouse Publishers, [2018] | Includes bibliographical references.
Identifiers: LCCN 2018036001 (print) | LCCN 2018038747 (ebook) | ISBN 9781625311696 (ebook) | ISBN 9781625311689 (pbk. : alk. paper)
Subjects: LCSH: Reading comprehension—Study and teaching (Elementary) | Reading (Elementary) | Picture books for children. | Children—Books and reading.
Classification: LCC LB1573.7 (ebook) | LCC LB1573.7 .B73 2018 (print) | DDC 372.47—dc23
LC record available at https://lccn.loc.gov/2018036001

Cover design by Peter H. Reynolds
Interior design by Jill Shaffer
Typesetting by Eclipse Publishing Services

Manufactured in the United States of America

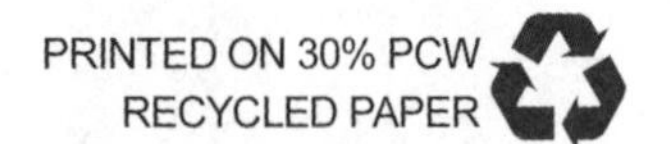

25 24 23 22 21 20 19 9 8 7 6 5 4 3 2

To all the giants, some known and some unknown, on whose shoulders I stand. And to all the family and friends who have supported me so that I could stay on those shoulders long enough to look around, take it all in, and create something meaningful.

Contents

Foreword

by Dr. Mary Howard

When I was a child, my favorite toy was an amazing ball of surprises from TG&Y. I still recall my childhood delight as I enthusiastically ripped through layers of paper strings intricately entwined around that little ball of surprises. I imagined the amazing goodies tucked lovingly inside, and my excitement escalated with each joyful unraveling.

Three years ago, I felt the same sense of joyful anticipation when I met Trevor Bryan and began an exciting journey of discovery into his brainchild, the Art of Comprehension (AoC). I was instantly intrigued that an art teacher viewed comprehension with such high esteem, and the more I learned about AoC, the more my enthusiasm grew. Each phase of my learning felt akin to that sense of childhood delight as I began the joyful unraveling of layers of goodies tucked lovingly inside the AoC process.

My enthusiasm escalated on June 24, 2016, when Trevor started a Voxer group to deepen our understanding. Using an image from Peter H. Reynolds's *The Dot* (2003), he asked us to share what we saw. First, narrow noticings of "I see drawings" were met with respectful probing that gently nudged me to new thinking. Slowly, what seemed invisible became visible as I began to make connections I never imagined. This was followed by Homer Winslow's *At the Window*, a painting displayed at the Princeton University Art Museum. As an art novice, I was amazed by the discoveries I was able to make with Trevor's encouragement. As my confidence grew, he masterfully stepped aside in a gradual release at its finest so that I could forge my own path toward unraveling new layers of meaning AoC style.

This engaging Voxer collaboration offered an insider's view of AoC in which we assumed the role of a learner reawakening a previously dormant spirit of awareness. I was struck by the entry point offered by AoC for striving and beginning readers, inspired that we began this process as striving beginners and yet felt completely successful. As Trevor explains, "Since pictures are easier to decode than written texts, reading pictures enables students to focus more on high-level comprehension and meaning-making." Having lived this firsthand, his words came to life in a very personal way.

But decoding images is only one layer of AoC. Using images to unlock new possibilities affords a powerful stepping-stone to words in a meaning-making merger that deepens understanding. Beginning with the familiar builds a thinking bridge that leads to success for every child no matter what that child brings to the literacy table. Initial anchor texts are used again and again as patterns emerge when students notice commonalities across texts as they strengthen comprehension. Trevor wisely extends this process to writer's craft in a celebration of the reciprocal nature of reading and writing. As we peel back layer after intricate layer of AoC, new possibilities for learners rise to the surface.

Using a wide range of beautiful picture books, artwork, and varied print sources, AoC offers a rich structure that actively engages students in a celebratory process of inquiry. Through supportive dialogue, they are immersed in a learning experience that models deep appreciation for talk that revolves around beautiful texts and images. There is no right or wrong answer or fear of reprisal—rather an invitational beckoning of ideas within conversations that nurture a thinking pathway. Intentionally thoughtful ponderings at just the right moments invite children into shared collaborations as we wait in the wings to gently nudge them to new understanding. We can then gradually relinquish support to give students time and space to bring a depth of meaning that happens naturally when we build a strong framework and then trust them to take ownership of their own thinking.

It is my honor to wholeheartedly endorse *The Art of Comprehension*. Having lived the AoC experience, I believe that this book needs to be in the hands of teachers everywhere. AoC expands our view of texts by creating an invisible thread that stretches across varied professional contexts to connect art, literacy, and all content areas. This broader view of texts has the potential to pave the way for a professional common ground where comprehension, conversations, and student-centered thinking can transform our frame of reference. As Trevor said in our first Voxer learning journey, "Art is an active sport," and in this sport, we can engage students in robust and joyful conversations where student thinking is honored along the way to new meaning in the company of others.

Let the games begin!

Acknowledgments

I trace the origins of the Art of Comprehension (AoC) to three significant moments in my life. The first happened around 1987 while I was sitting on the rug listening to my sixth-grade teacher Mrs. Marino, read *Bridge to Terabithia* (Paterson 1977). The second happened a few years later while I was listening to an audio tour narrated by comedian Steve Martin for a Picasso exhibit at the Metropolitan Museum of Art. And the third took place around 1999 during my first back-to-school night as an art teacher. Although this is not the arena to share the specifics of these events, I wanted to mention them to show that the evolution of the AoC has taken place over a course of decades. During that time, I have been influenced and supported by numerous people. It would be impossible for me to mention all of them. And so, although the following list of people may be somewhat substantial, please know that it is by no means complete. My sincerest apologies to anyone who I have left off this list.

First, to the principal (who shall not be named) who decided not to renew my contract: when one door closes, other doors open.

To the Jackson Township School District, which opened its doors for me: I am grateful for the support that has been given to me over the past fifteen years.

To Donna Donner and Justin Dolcimascolo: What can I say? Without your friendship AoC never would have grown wings.

So thankful for our time together. I will always cherish our journey. To my former principal (and current assistant superintendent), Daniel Baginski: Thank you for encouraging me to follow and explore my interests and ideas. Your early support was invaluable.

I'd also like to thank all of the other Jackson Township administrators who have supported me over the last several years. Much thanks to Theresa Licitra, Dr. Lisa Lane, Michael Burgos, Tim Harrison, Sean Levinson, and Liz Villecco.

To my colleagues Jill Villecco, Danielle Parella, Jessica Tice, Katy Bischoff, and Sandra Morales: Thank you for answering so many questions and for always making me feel welcome in your classrooms.

To my colleagues Kristi Rutyna and Sharon Lokerson: Thanks for storing so much of my stuff.

To my colleagues Alyssa Agoston, Dana Bellino, April Brucculeri, Melissa Barnfield, Cindy Cooney, Gail Conley, Natalie Cortez, Carl Danish, Tiffany Garnett, Judy Guedes, Maryanne Hreha, Colleen, Hussa, Jason Liebman, Sue Longo, Rebecca Marin, Carol O'Brien, Nick Paradise, Kyle Perrine, Lori Rudenjack, Sherri Sulia, and Kathy Williams: Thanks for helping to make Elms a great place to show up to all of these years.

To my colleagues Emily Clark, Maria Martinez, Jamie Lee, Lia Thomas, and Jennifer Quick: Thanks for all of the support you've given me over the last several years.

To Brice Batchelor Hall and Allegra D'Adamo: Thanks for helping me to bring my work into the Princeton University Art Museum. I'm grateful for each conversation about the artworks that AoC has spurred.

To all of my students: Thanks for the courage to share so much of yourselves, you've taught me more than I ever could have imagined.

To Brooke Geller: Thanks for taking my work seriously and for helping me to start to share it.

To Christopher Lehman: Thanks so much for your early support. Your writing advice and encouragement were invaluable.

To Dr. Mary Howard: Your generosity and passion for children and teaching is inspiring. Thanks for always sharing your voice. It has positively impacted so many . . . including me.

To Joan Moser and Kari Yates: Thanks for believing in me, for championing my work, and for helping me find and share my voice.

To the Voxer cousins, Joanne Duncan, Katheryn Hoffmann-Thompson, Jan Burkins, Fran McVeigh, Jenn Hayhurst, Jill DeRosa, Dani Burtsfield, Susie Rolander, Christina Nosek, Erica Pecorale, Jennifer Sniadecki, Julieanne Harmatz, Lisa Eickholdt, Margaret Simon: Thanks for your ongoing support, inspiration, wisdom, and friendship. Love singing with this choir.

To Rich Czyz: Hard to believe that we went from locked closets to Four O'clock Faculty. It's been one heck of a ride. Long live Marth!

To Sue Slavin and the late Erica Steinbauer: Thanks for listening. Your early support meant a lot!

To Peter and Paul Reynolds: Thanks for believing in my mission and supporting me to help make my mark. I hope it inspires and enables others to make theirs.

To Kyle Stevenson: Thanks for helping to bring my story to life. Your illustrations are beautiful. So grateful that you continue to be part of my creative life.

To Wally Bilotta: Your help organizing the visuals for this book has been tremendous. I can't thank you enough. Appreciate the great headshots, too!

To Stenhouse and my editors, Tori Bachman, Bill Varner, Louisa A. Irele, Stephanie Levy, and Brian Evan-Jones: I am so grateful for this opportunity to share my work. Thanks for your ongoing patience, guidance, and support.

To my in-laws, Bob and Ellie Pritchard: Thanks for your ongoing support of all my creative endeavors.

To my in-laws, Cy and Barbara Borretsky: Thanks for always supporting my creative life.

To my aunt, Bonnie Greaves: From shows to exhibits to discussions, thanks for supporting and adding so much to my creative life over the years.

To my brother and sister-in-law, Jeff and Dana Bryan: Thanks for always supporting my creative work. It's meant more than you know.

To my Mom and Dad, Larry and Helen Bryan: Thanks for relentlessly supporting me throughout my creative journeys and for always believing in my artwork, regardless of the form.

And to my family, Laura, Hanna, and Owen: Your patience and support have been beyond measure. Thanks so much for giving me space to create. We did it!

If great books are great works of art, then reading is a form of art appreciation and writing is a form of art creation. From this stance, literacy teachers are really art teachers without the smocks or carts or dirty, stained hands.

Introduction

I think one of the gifts of this work is that it is opening [students'] eyes to the amazing deep thinking that they are capable of—and whether that transfers now or later, the important thing is they now see themselves as kids who can think deeply and grow their ideas through conversation. That's pretty huge!

Kathryn Hoffmann-Thompson

Fourth- to sixth-grade teacher, Pine Point School

White Earth Reservation, Minnesota

I **want to start** by sharing a conversation that I had during a family day tour at the Princeton University Art Museum while showing a group of children and adults a landscape painting by William Merritt Chase (Figure I.1).

I asked the group to list everything that they could see. The parents and children, siblings and friends worked as partners, using the common English language arts (ELA) practice of turning-and-talking. After about thirty seconds, I asked my first question, an easy one:

"Where are the girls?"

I waited. Slowly hands began to rise.

"You can call it out," I said.

Most, if not all, of the viewers agreed that the girls were in a field by the sea.

"What could they be doing?" I asked next. I was hoping that the group could make some inferences and use specific evidence from the picture to support their thinking. They did. Hands went up again. I called on a boy of about eight.

"Looking for flowers," he said.

"Why does that make sense?" I asked. "Tell your partner."

The partners discussed the foliage with the little spots of color and the girls, with their heads tilted down, engrossed in their looking.

FIGURE I.1
William Merritt Chase, Landscape: Shinnecock, Long Island, *ca. 1896. Gift of Francis A. Comstock, Princeton University Art Museum.*

After a few moments of discussion, I asked another question. "What else could they be doing?"

"Looking for shells," a mom offered.

"And why does that answer also make sense to all of us?" Again, the group quickly supported their thinking by mentioning the sea, the sand, and the posture of the girls. When pressed a bit further, they used their background knowledge of shelling at the shore to support their thinking.

I asked one more time. "What else could they be doing?" It became quiet. The group searched the artwork and their schema for clues. Finally, a tiny voice piped up. It was a little girl with curly brown hair in the arms of her mother.

"What did you say?" I asked.

"Looking for bugs," she repeated. Sounds of realization arose from the group. I got goose bumps. This little girl not only had brought her background knowledge to this picture but also had broadened the thinking of everyone looking at the painting.

We went on to discuss the mood of this picture. "Why would these girls be happy?" I asked. The group discussed how the girls were at the beach, how it was a pleasant day, how they were dressed up, and how they all looked engaged.

I then asked, "Could any of these girls be a bit sad?"

Again I heard the small voice that belonged to the curly-haired little girl. "That girl," she said pointing to the girl alone in the foreground.

"And why do you think she might be sad?"

"Because no one is playing with her."

"Did you ever feel that way?" Her curls bounced up and down as she nodded.

"When?" I asked.

"When my cousins wouldn't play with me."

During the few minutes that we discussed the small painting, the little girl in her mother's arms had engaged in a huge range of higher-order thinking. She had made inferences based on textural evidence, stretched her thinking, used her schema, expressed empathy for one of the characters, explored different points of view, *and* made a meaningful text-to-self connection.

At the end of the discussion, I asked the mother her daughter's age. Her response? "Three and a half." Remarkable. At three and a half, this little girl was thinking like a reader, exhibiting the kind of thinking found in good ELA classrooms.

It's easy to imagine that, if this little girl could participate in discussions like this on a regular basis, by the time she was in upper elementary school, her ability to dissect and discuss texts in complex ways would be enviable. She would be able not only to think about her world in meaningful ways but also to help others do the same.

Whether working with young children or older children, striving students or soaring students, this is the type of thinking and discussion that the Art of Comprehension (AoC) can bring to your classroom. AoC does this by providing simple yet effective tools that help students find, develop, and share their voice. Furthermore, students can learn to use these tools first with visual texts, which are highly accessible and easy to manage. This enables all learners, striving readers and nonreaders included, to join classroom conversations—building their confidence as well as community.

Leland Jacobs (1965, 2) wrote, "In books for young children, pictures are important." Since then, numerous literacy education giants, such as Lucy Calkins (Calkins and Franco 2015), Gail Boushey and Joan

Moser (2014), Katie Wood Ray (2010), and Jan Burkins and Kim Yaris (2018) have echoed the sentiment that illustrations certainly have a place in ELA classrooms. But even with this long-held belief and the rise of visual literacy, very little literature exists regarding how to explicitly teach students to engage meaningfully with and make meaning of visual texts. AoC helps to fill this void. What's more, my colleagues and I realized that by teaching students to engage meaningfully with visual texts, we are better positioned to help them to engage with written texts, both when they read and when they write.

You might initially think this book is about visual literacy, and you wouldn't be completely wrong. Using the approach explained in *The Art of Comprehension* will certainly improve your students' ability to think about and discuss visual images and other visual texts. During my many conversations about artworks and illustrations, I've had numerous goose bump moments when students shared simple astonishing ideas or, even better, when a striving or normally silent student opened up, without prompting, to become an active and integral part of a classroom discussion. I cherish those moments and relish the fact that they have been fairly common over the past few years.

However, because AoC was originally structured around comprehension strategies and the newer ELA standards, using this approach will improve your students' thinking and conversations around *all* texts, including written texts. So, instead, think of *The Art of Comprehension* not as a book about visual literacy but as a book about literacy with an expanded view of what constitutes text.

The International Literacy Association defines literacy as, "the ability to identify, understand, interpret, create, compute, and communicate using visual, audible, and digital materials across disciplines and in any context" (https://www.literacyworldwide.org/about-us/why-literacy). This stance broadens the older, more traditional, view of literacy, which focused only on the reading and writing of written texts. It recognizes that, to be literate today, students have to learn to manage texts that take many forms. This book takes that same stance. To meet the demands of today and tomorrow, our idea of what a text is has to grow.

For many, expanding the idea of what a text is complicates ELA instruction. How can ELA educators become experts in all the various forms of communication that students are expected to read and create? Furthermore, while demands on ELA teachers and students have increased, their instructional time often has not. This book aims to provide some relief, not because it has all of the answers but because it cuts through some of the clutter: what Ralph Fletcher refers to in his book *Joy Write* (2017, 7) as "that weighty cargo" that ELA teachers have been asked to teach in recent years. Although Fletcher was talking specifically about writing, it's fair to say that weighty cargo has been added to all aspects of literacy instruction. Teachers and students have a lot to lug around. *The Art of Comprehension* outlines a simple way to begin to help students engage the sophisticated work that they have to do and sort through some of the cargo with a manageable and practical approach that is appropriate for all learners. AoC accomplishes this in three key ways.

First, although AoC takes an expanded view of what a text is, it focuses on the similarities between texts, not their differences. The tools of AoC provide a consistent approach that help students to begin to transact with nearly any fictional or informational text: a movie, a documentary, a TV show, a play, an artwork, an illustration, a poem, an article, a graphic novel, or a novel. AoC offers consistency that acts as a stabilizing force that helps teachers and students move forward with confidence.

Second, AoC draws clear connections between comprehension and craft, so that at times it merges reading and writing instruction. When students are using the tools of AoC to explore the texts they are reading, the tools also help them to see how the texts were crafted. For example, with the tools in hand, or at least in mind, students can more easily see that the textual evidence that they pull from the texts they read is the same kind of information and detail that they need to put into the texts they write. This creates efficiency, which allows ELA teachers to capitalize on their limited instructional time.

Last, AoC provides an authentic, age-appropriate approach to meeting the new higher ELA standards. By broadening our view of text to include visual images, we can provide more manageable and engaging texts to more students. This allows younger students to engage with the higher standards earlier, providing them more time and experiences with them. It also provides nonreaders and striving readers with rich, authentic opportunities to practice and learn the forms of thinking that strong comprehension requires even if they struggle with decoding written texts.

Essentially, this book has three parts. In the beginning, I will share the tools of the trade. These three components of AoC will help you and your students implement the approach quickly. They are simple, but like so many simple tools, they are extremely helpful. We'll begin to explore these tools the same way I help my students to start to use them, through visual texts. Next, I will show you how these tools can be used with written texts. Finally, we'll explore how these tools can support students when they work on their own writing.

I sincerely hope you enjoy this book. Like the many students who have sat before me, I'm excited to share my thinking. Roaming through visual and written texts with my students, exploring and discovering the ideas they hold and the ideas they inspire, letting them guide us down previously unknown paths into unimaginable territory have created some of the greatest moments not just of my teaching career but of my life. It's exciting work for sure. I hope this approach can help open up exciting new pathways forward for you and your students, too.

Enjoy the journey!

CHAPTER 1

Looking at the Familiar

If great books are great works of art, then reading is a form of art appreciation and writing is a form of art creation. From this stance, literacy teachers are really art teachers without the smocks or carts or dirty, stained hands.

Trevor Bryan

Think about sadness for a second.

Now think about describing sadness through writing.

You could write something like this:

A frown formed on his face. His shoulders slumped.

An illustrator can provide the same information, by drawing something like Figure 1.1.

The information in the writing and the illustration is the same; it's simply presented differently. We could discuss all of the ways they are different, but I'd like to focus on just one: the drawing is

FIGURE 1.1
Illustrations can provide the same information as written texts and can be independently decoded and comprehended by nonreaders, striving readers, and beginning readers.

decodable for students who can't decode written text. For me, this is the most interesting and important difference because the ability to decode the illustration creates space for these students to think about it, work with it, and discuss it. For example, viewing illustrations can help very young students, nonreaders, striving readers, as well as readers to do the following:

- ✔ Pull key details out of the illustration
- ✔ Infer and synthesize what key details mean
- ✔ Summarize
- ✔ Make predictions
- ✔ Support their thinking with textual evidence
- ✔ Determine themes and big ideas
- ✔ Discuss symbolism
- ✔ Identify key moments in stories
- ✔ Compare/contrast
- ✔ Make connections
- ✔ Notice story structure

This is the work of strong readers: work that our students need to do but work that can be challenging to teach. The Art of Comprehension (AoC) provides an easy and efficient approach that can help all students develop the skills to do this work.

At this point, you may be thinking, *Well, I don't know anything about art or viewing pictures! How am I possibly going to help my students to do this?* Don't worry! I know you can help your students because reading an illustration and reading written text are more similar than you may think. Both essentially consist of two parts: decoding and comprehending. Since pictures are easier to decode than written texts, reading pictures enables students to focus more on high-level comprehension and meaning-making.

To get a bit of a feel for how this works, take a moment to explore the picture in Figure 1.2. Then try to answer these questions:

- What's the mood?
- How do you know what the mood is?
- What's causing the mood?

These questions may sound simplistic, but they get at the heart of this illustration. More important, these questions get at the heart

FIGURE 1.2
The opening illustration from The Dot *by Peter H. Reynolds*

of the story. They reflect what the story is about. Therefore, if students can answer these questions, they are right *in* the story. AoC gives students the tools they need to answer these questions with confidence. The tools help students notice key details, such as her downward eyebrow; her crossed arms; the muted colors; the quiet, empty classroom; and the blank paper; these details are easily missed but help students to think about and discuss the picture deeply. Furthermore, the tools and skills students use to explore and discuss this picture meaningfully can be brought to other texts, including written texts. Pictures provide a means to help all learners develop the skills and confidence they need for strong comprehension and robust conversations.

SIMPLE STARTS

The picture in Figure 1.2 is the opening illustration from the book *The Dot* by Peter H. Reynolds (2003). It's the first picture that I share with students and teachers when I introduce them to AoC. I use this book first because the story is mostly and clearly communicated through the simple illustrations. This makes the story accessible to a wide range of learners, including nonreaders, struggling readers, and English language learners. However, the story's themes are also sophisticated, which allows rich, deep conversations to grow around it. This makes it appropriate for my soaring learners, too.

The book's simplicity also lets students acquire tremendous command over it. Students can quickly absorb the story's moods and mood structure and grasp how they were crafted. The illustrations are easy to recall, allowing us to refer to them throughout the year as we tackle more complex texts or explore a new writing concept.

Having an anchor text that can be referred to often enables students to put the new, more challenging information into a context that helps them to easily sort it out and organize it in their minds. An anchor text helps students create a mental model of how stories work, which helps students to manage, to explore, and to understand new and unfamiliar territories (Edwards-Leis 2012), including new and unfamiliar texts.

Now let's look more closely at how the illustration in Figure 1.2 can help students to engage and develop some of the reading skills listed earlier.

IDENTIFYING KEY DETAILS

Good readers note important details that help them make meaning of text, as demonstrated in Chris Lehman and Kate Roberts's techniques for reading closely for text evidence. They write that students need to "choose specific details to gather as data" (2014, 12). Like writers, illustrators and other visual artists also put key information into their work, and nonreaders and striving readers can practice identifying key information in a text by viewing illustrations. In Figure 1.2, when students notice Vashti's furrowed brow, slumped body, crossed arms, isolation, and the colors that envelop her, they are identifying specific details that aid comprehension. Viewing illustrations and other visual images is an excellent way for students to practice identifying key details and fitting them together to form a pattern in order to construct meaning.

MAKING INFERENCES

When discussing complex texts in *What Readers Really Do*, Dorothy Barnhouse and Vicki Vinton write: "What is often most complex about these texts is what is most invisible, i.e. places that require a reader to infer" (2012, 69). When viewers read illustrations, especially if they are not paired with words (but often even when they are), viewers have to make inferences based on the information provided by the artist. For instance, even within the written text, Peter H. Reynolds (2003) never directly states that Vashti is upset, frustrated, or, as one first grader wrote, "Duschrest" (distressed). Instead, viewers must infer her mood based on the evidence Reynolds provides. Artists show information, they don't tell it, which is why viewing is a wonderful way to help readers learn about and practice inferring. Likewise, viewing is also a great way to explore the concept of showing versus telling information in writing. As readers, students make inferences on information that is shown. As writers, students enable their readers to make inferences when they show. Whether students are reading or writing, AoC guides students toward the kind of information they need to think about in order to make reasonable inferences.

DETERMINING THEMES, MAIN IDEAS, AND BIG IDEAS

"Identifying the theme or main idea is something else students should always practice" (Boyles 2014, 104). Any text, poem, article, essay, or novel has a theme, a main idea, or a big idea. This is true for artwork, too. Photographs, paintings, sculptures, and illustrations always have to be about something. Therefore, students can begin identifying themes, main ideas, and big ideas through viewing visual texts such as illustrations. For instance, the big idea behind the illustration from *The Dot* (see Figure 1.2) may be expressed as "Schoolwork can be frustrating" or "Sometimes we feel stuck" or "Not knowing what to do can feel lonely." But even if students can only use a single word, such as *frustration, sadness*, or *loneliness* to express what this picture is about, it still puts them on a solid path toward the more complex work regarding theme.

MAKING CONNECTIONS

Kylene Beers and Robert Probst write, "The most rigorous reading is to find out what those words on that page mean to our own lives" (2013, 42). They are talking about readers making text-to-self connections.

Making connections has long been touted as an important comprehension strategy that good readers do as they read. Irene Fountas and Gay Su Pinnell state, "Readers constantly search for connections between what they already know and what they encounter in text" (2001, 316). Students, including young students, nonreaders, and striving readers, can begin this practice by making strong connections to illustrations. Students might create a text-to-self connection with the Reynolds illustration in Figure 1.2 by thinking about times in their own lives when they have felt frustrated or stuck just as Vashti does. And when students make meaningful connections that help them understand characters and the story, they are not only building comprehension skills but also generating possible story ideas for their own writing (or artwork).

NOTICING SYMBOLISM

Understanding symbolism in stories is a crucial part of understanding any art form, whether written or visual. "When you teach students to notice symbols, you teach them to pay closer attention to texts [visual or written]" (Calkins and Robb 2014, 105). Viewing illustrations allows students to start exploring the meaning of objects, settings, or characters in this way. Even the youngest students I work with understand that Vashti's blank paper can symbolize her frustration or emptiness. When I asked a group of first graders why the paper can symbolize how Vashti feels, one boy explained, "Because the paper is empty just like her!" As the story progresses, students can identify how her paper transforms from a symbol of frustration into a symbol of joy, creativity, and confidence, and these same students can easily discuss how her teacher was a symbol of hope and support.

BUILDING COMMUNITY

In the introduction, I mentioned a quote by Leland Jacobs. I'd like to share a little more of what he wrote to introduce my next point: "In books for young children, the pictures are important. In fact, the illustrations are integral in the total contents of the book" (Jacobs 1965, 2). Jacobs then goes on to describe the role of pictures in informational books, "mood" literature, poetry, and fiction. He concludes the section on pictures by stating, "In the most enjoyable literature for children, a harmony of print and pictures is achieved. One can read the pictures right along with the print. Or one can read the print through the pictures" (3).

As the 1965 Jacobs quote makes clear, accessing the content of books through pictures is not new, and, as I also mentioned in the introduction, it is still recommended by literacy gurus of today. It's an idea that I totally support. However, if our use of pictures is only focused on supporting access to content, then we neglect another, perhaps more important, role that meaningful engagement with pictures and illustrations can play: it can help *all* students to become active and engaged members of the classroom community. For me, this has been one of the most rewarding aspects of AoC.

The first day that I tried viewing a picture through a literacy lens was in the classroom of my friend and colleague Donna Donner. Her fourth-grade inclusion class was made up of a wide range of learners, including several striving students who had trouble engaging with their reading work. Like Vashti, they were (metaphorically) turning their backs on the texts before them. Their book pages might as well have been blank.

Donna and I theorized that by replacing written text with a visual text—a simple illustration, which was far easier to decode—her striving students would be able to focus their cognitive energy on meaning-making and comprehension strategies. We further theorized that, given this chance to make meaning, her striving students would begin to contribute meaningfully to the rich conversations that played a prominent role in learning in her class.

As I showed the students that first picture, I looked for two things. First, to see whether students who normally didn't speak during class joined the conversation. And, second, to see whether these students could demonstrate comprehension skills. These were simple metrics but important ones. Donna and I knew that making these students feel that they were valued and contributing members of the classroom community could help them unlock their potential. We also knew that, if everyone felt comfortable sharing their thinking, we would all have more opportunities to learn. Sure enough, as I clumsily led a discussion based on a simple drawing of Snoopy and Woodstock hugging, we saw hands rise and heard voices speak that had previously stayed low and remained silent. Those striving students shared ideas and exhibited comprehension strategies. It was a start.

Although we didn't know it at the time, we were instinctively trying to help students engage with what I now refer to as the Core Four. The Core Four are four elements that students need access to in order to become active and confident members of the classroom community.

They are *texts, thinking, voice,* and *conversations*. Lacking one of these makes it impossible for students to reach their potential.

The Core Four isn't an exhaustive list, but the elements provide a clear way of organizing what I see when I fall short with some students as well as giving me a way to help them. For instance, if a student isn't responding to a picture or a written text, I'll work to find a good-fit picture or written text for that student to engage with. Or, if I am not hearing from a student, I'll figure out some alternative way for that student to use his voice to share his thinking.

Here is how AoC can help students access the Core Four.

Texts: Students need to be able to access the texts, whether visual or written, that they work with. This doesn't mean simply having a text in hand or having plenty of books in the classroom library. It means having a text that they can enter into, explore, and use to push their thinking. This is where the fun is, and fun means engagement. I want my students to be comprehension contortionists, bending and weaving their ideas in insanely interesting ways. AoC helps students to do this by providing entry points. It guides students toward useful information to find and track that helps them to unpack the meaning that the author, illustrator, or performer intended or that they can use to assign their own meaning. These first steps into a text can help them to progress from the meaning-making sidelines onto the meaning-making field. Furthermore, it helps them to think more broadly about texts, moving from answering questions about texts to asking questions about the texts.

Thinking: Even students who answer general questions correctly can have difficulty explaining or proving why their answers make sense. The components of AoC, which I share and explain in the following chapters, help students to access their thinking by providing a structure, tools, and vocabulary that are easy to use and can be widely and meaningfully applied. Everything about AoC is geared toward helping students make meaning. The components of AoC help students to organize both the text and their thinking around the text in a way that is helpful yet unrestrictive. This allows all students to bring their individual experiences and ideas to the text to make meaning.

Voice: AoC helps students find their voice by providing a vocabulary that students can use to express their thinking clearly around a written text, an image, or a performance. By using common language around shared experiences, it increases the likelihood that all students will be understood and can understand others, which can not only make conversations more meaningful and efficient but also help eliminate frustration for many students, including both those who have difficulty expressing themselves and those whose robust, far-reaching thinking isn't always understood by their peers.

Conversation: When students have access to relevant information in a text, access to their thinking around a text, and access to common language regarding that text, they have the essential components needed to join a meaningful classroom conversation, which gives them access to exponential learning. Therefore, AoC not only helps students to enter a text more confidently but also helps students enter the learning community. Varied and unique student voices engaged in exploratory conversations are the fuel that feeds the engine of excitement, and nothing beats walking into an exciting classroom.

AoC certainly hasn't solved all of our students' problems, but for many, AoC has given them a point of access—a chance to get off the bench and into the game—or provided a valuable scaffold, allowing them to take their game to new heights. As Debbie Miller points out, "Real communities flourish when we can bring together the voices, hearts and souls of the people who inhabit them" (2002, 17). AoC can help to do just this.

THE MAGIC OF MOOD

You may have noticed that *mood* has shown up a few times in this chapter (as well as in the introduction). *Mood* is by far my favorite word to use when discussing meaning-making and comprehension because stories are told through mood. Mood is what makes them resonate with the audience. As humans, we are highly sensitive to others' emotional states. It is our understanding of moods that help us to connect with one another, often deeply. Moods also drive our own lives. If you think about the most significant moments of your life, chances are these moments are swathed in mood and emotion. As a result, artists, performers, and writers take advantage of our propensity to respond to moods by infusing them into their work. Therefore, determining mood is the simplest, most straightforward way for our students, striving learners and nonreaders alike, to enter into most quality, good-fit text regardless of form or genre.

A fun example of the use of mood to drive a story is the movie *Jaws*. Take the theme music (Williams 1975), I'm sure most of you know it, and if you do, then go ahead and hum it. How do you feel? Even as I write, sitting in my safe, comfortable kitchen, humming the theme music to *Jaws*, it's hard for me not to feel a bit of tension caused by images of a menacing beast swimming through my house, lurking in the shadows and getting ready to feast. That's the power of well-crafted moods. We *feel them deeply* even if we *know* they are fictitious and ridiculous.

As educators, we can take advantage of our students' innate ability to recognize and connect to moods, because effective texts, just like *Jaws* or the most significant moments of our lives, are dominated by powerful moods. The end of a great story, essay or article, song or poem, screenplay or speech, well crafted and well written, will leave us feeling something. Great texts resonate with us emotionally and often reverberate well after the book is closed, after the applause ends, or after the credits roll.

Whether the people or places we are reading about are real or imagined, it's through moods that we connect, just like in our own lives. This is true for both written and visual texts. If students can determine the moods within a text using the evidence the text provides, that's a good indication that students comprehend the information before them.

Determining or inferring the mood is also where comprehension and craft intersect. Moods have to be crafted, so in order to determine the mood, students have to explore *how* it was crafted. When students determine the moods and track those moods over the course of a text, they not only comprehend the story but also think about story structure and presentation. And understanding how moods are crafted and presented in the texts they read (including visual texts) is crucial to students when they want to create their *own* written work that will resonate strongly with *their* intended audiences.

When we encourage our students to wade into the moods created by authors and artists, we help them to experience entering into a piece more fully. We give them a way to think about and discuss the text deeply and meaningfully. Students, even striving students and very young students, can understand mood and what is causing that mood; when they do, they not only gain an understanding of the piece in both content and craft they also can begin to connect to it and hold on to it in authentic ways.

In this chapter, I shared some reasons why focusing on visual texts can benefit students in ELA classrooms. In Chapter 2, I'll share the first component of AoC, the Access Lenses, a tool that was a game changer for my colleagues and me. It will help you with how to start providing the explicit instruction around visual texts that your students need. This tool can improve your students' work around written texts and their writing, too.

CHAPTER 2

The Access Lenses

The following passage was written by Jackson, a fifth-grade student from Justin Dolcimascolo's class, after thinking about and discussing the painting in Figure 2.1 using the Art of Comprehension (AoC) to access it:

FIGURE 2.1
John Frederick Kensett, Lake George, *ca. 1870. Bequest of Elaine King in memory of her husband, Col. Herbert G. King, Princeton University Art Museum.*

I think a universal theme of this picture is that life can be rugged and sometimes rough but still beautiful. In this picture, the mountains are pointy and sharp and represent the rough parts of life; the lake represents the calm, peaceful parts. Even though the sky looks gloomy and cloudy, there is still a bit of sunshine peeking through, ready to brighten up the landscape. There are also bits of blue sky which represent optimism.

The painting makes me think of Lemony Snicket's A Series of Unfortunate Events. The dark mountain makes me think of Count Olaf, the main villain, who is determined to harm the Baudelaire children. Even when things seem perilous for the children, they somehow find their way to get to the blue part of the sky.

I can connect to the universal theme of this painting in many ways. I have a chronic health condition that I don't usually talk about but feel that in this case it really applies. My health condition is like the big ominous mountain with its twists and turns and rough spots. I don't ever want the mountain to take over the whole picture. I remember to look for the peaceful, happy places too, like the lake, and the blue sky. Even when my health is challenged, I try to look at the bright side of things.

Just like the conversation involving the three-and-a-half-year-old, discussed in the introduction, Jackson's response captures the richness of the conversations that I frequently have with students around artworks and other kinds of visual texts. Although this writing is from a number of years ago, it is still one of my favorite responses ever because, as I have stressed in the introduction and in Chapter 1, it demonstrates so clearly that when an artwork or visual text is treated similarly to a written text, viewers can use the same forms of thinking that help readers when they are reading.

Through his writing, Jackson was able to do the following:

- ✔ Determine universal theme: life is a mixture of rough parts and bright parts
- ✔ Identify moods: rough, gloom, bright, calm, peaceful, optimism
- ✔ Gather and cite specific textural evidence: calm water, sharp mountains, cloudy skies, and bright parts
- ✔ Discuss symbolism and view artwork (text) metaphorically: mountains as rough parts of life, the lake as the calm parts of life, and sunshine as optimism
- ✔ Make a text-to-text connection: connecting components of the painting to characters from the book series A Series of Unfortunate Events

- ✔ Make a text-to-self connection: used both texts as launching pads for reflection on his own life: connected the painting and book characters to his own struggles in life and his response to those struggles
- ✔ Clearly share (present) an idea for others to reflect on and perhaps grow from: try to look for the bright spots

As I've already argued, by expanding our view of what text is, we open up opportunities for all of our students to engage in the forms of thinking that they need for academic success. Treating illustrations as texts can help all students to practice authentic meaning-making, which is the whole goal of reading. However, just as explicit instruction helps students with reading written texts, explicit instruction also helps students engage with visual texts. What does explicit instruction around visual texts look like? The rest of this chapter begins to answer this question.

THE ACCESS LENSES

The Access Lenses make up the first component of AoC, and I consider them to be the heart of it (see Figure 2.2). They are the glue, the lynchpin, the keystone. Regardless of the metaphor, the Access Lenses make it much easier for you and your students to enter into visual texts (and eventually written texts) and to think about and discuss them deeply and meaningfully.

The Access Lenses also spurred a remarkable transformation with the classes I worked with when I was starting to develop AoC. With the Access Lenses in hand, students became active explorers and meaning-makers, instead of passive question answerers. As a result, my classrooms became more student centered. Students were able to discover information within visual and written texts, independently or with partners, and they were more likely to synthesize the information they found in unique and surprising ways, creating lots of space for discussion and growth. The classroom became more exciting for everyone, and with this excitement came engagement and joyful learning. Students jumped into texts and felt like explorers, always on the brink of discovery. Most important, with the Access Lenses, every learner had a chance to make the next big discovery. Providing students with the Access Lenses is like giving students a golden ticket that grants them access to the Core Four (texts, thinking, voice, and conversations) discussed in Chapter 1.

There are nine Access Lenses. The first three are the most common and, therefore, in some ways, the easiest to introduce and to use.

FIGURE 2.2
The Access Lenses are the heart of AoC.

However, just as Irene Fountas and Gay Su Pinnell encourage using multiple comprehension strategies concurrently (2001, 345), I don't encourage using the Access Lenses in isolation. I highlight the first three lenses only because, for some striving students, focusing on these three can be helpful if they are having trouble taking their first step. But again, I strongly encourage you to help all of your students consider all of the lenses as much as possible because each lens can open up new paths into the text, into their thinking, and help expand their voices.

LENS 1: FACIAL EXPRESSION (FACES)

This is the easiest lens for students to start using. Facial expressions reveal a lot about a character's moods and are generally easy for even young children to understand. However, interpreting facial expressions still needs to be explicitly taught because even older, capable students often have trouble using text evidence to support their thinking. Many students can say, "I know that the character is upset" but have trouble adding, "*because he is frowning.*" The facial expressions lens can help many students enter a text and begin to use textual evidence to support their thinking. In addition, since characters' facial expressions often change throughout a story, the facial expression lens provides students a simple way to start to identify patterns that authors and illustrators establish and to understand the changes in patterns, which helps them to track a character's development and notice key moments.

LENS 2: BODY LANGUAGE, ACTION/INACTION (BODIES)

The body language lens often goes hand in hand with the facial expression lens. If a face looks excited, the body will usually look excited, too. As with facial expressions, most students are capable of making inferences based on reading either a character's body language or a character's action or inaction. Pairing information delivered through faces and bodies is also another straightforward way to introduce students to patterns. For instance, if the face looks happy and the body looks happy, then there is a pattern. Once a pattern is established, you can ask your students (or students can ask themselves), *What else fits the pattern to support the mood?* The other lenses can guide students toward where to look to answer this question, which helps them use textual evidence to support their thinking. By doing this work, we can also begin to teach students that, when the pattern changes, it usually indicates an important part or key moment of the story.

LENS 3: COLORS

From approaching storm clouds, to flushed cheeks, to dark rooms, to fireworks, to flowers bursting beneath sunny skies, the colors lens pops up everywhere. Colors are often used to convey moods, and, once again, even very young children can grasp this idea. Getting students accustomed to thinking about how colors are used to reflect moods is a simple way to promote deeper thinking about images, texts, and performances. Discussing how colors are used to create and convey moods is also an easy way to discuss symbolism and metaphors (see Lens 9).

LENS 4: CLOSE TOGETHER, FAR APART LENS

Characters' proximity to, or distance from, people, places, or objects can indicate how they are feeling, what they want, or the predicament they are in. It's not just physical proximity that can be considered using this lens; students can also think about emotional proximity. For instance, although characters may be right next to one another, they may be light-years apart emotionally. Think of two people sitting next to each other on a subway or siblings sitting in the back seat during a long, difficult car ride!

LENS 5: ALONE

As with the close together, far apart lens, the alone lens can relate to both physical and emotional aloneness. In addition, when characters are alone, it may cause them to feel isolated and lonely, or isolation may be a positive experience, a cause for feeling calm or reflective. Either way, when characters are alone in visual or in written texts, their isolation needs to be considered in regards to the mood or moods the artist or writer is crafting.

LENS 6: WORDS OR NO WORDS/SOUNDS OR SILENCE

The words that characters say, as well as other sounds expressed within a text, often reveal much about what is happening. What characters say and how they say it provides important information about thoughts, feelings, and motivations, just as the soft lapping of waves or the rumbling of thunder can give a reader or viewer an indication of what's happening or what's to come. And when characters don't speak or sounds are not heard, we often can learn just as much. Silence can speak volumes.

Although viewers don't always think about pictures having sound, the idea isn't as complicated as you may think. For example, imagine a boy by himself drawing. Quiet is implied, right? Now, picture an illustration of students at recess. Not as quiet, is it?

LENS 7: BIG THINGS AND LITTLE THINGS

At times, authors and artists will explicitly state or show that something is big or little. For instance, in many picture books, key moments or climaxes are depicted on double-page layouts in which the scale indicates their importance. Awareness of the physical size of a character or a setting often helps readers comprehend the dynamics of a story. In *The BFG* by Roald Dahl (1982), the BFG's size compared to the other giants partially explains why he struggles to fit in.

The big and little things lens can also be applied to the emotional state or symbolic nature of characters. For instance, sometimes the *smallest* of gestures by one character, such as a squeeze of a hand or a devilish smirk, may have a *big* impact on another character.

LENS 8: ZOOMING IN OR OUT

Artists and authors will often zoom in or zoom out on scenes. What they choose to zoom in on frequently provides a key detail that they want their audience to notice. They also zoom out to give the audience a more complete picture of what their characters are experiencing. Thinking about how close-ups or panorama shots are used in movies to help tell the story is an easy way to understand this concept. A classic example is found in Westerns when two gunslingers face off in the center of town. The director will often zoom out to reveal the whole scene and then zoom in on the cowboys' eyes and fingers to help show the intense mood. However, these techniques aren't always used in such obvious ways, and sometimes, it's up to the audience to do this work themselves. For instance, the audience can zoom in on key details, such as eyebrows, hands, colors, or objects, which can clue them into the mood of the scene or provide a hint about what might be coming in the future.

LENS 9: SYMBOLS AND METAPHORS

As I discussed in Chapter 1, humans are very good at understanding the symbolic nature of things. When I introduce students to the idea of thinking about objects, settings, actions, and characters as symbols, I have them focus on two things: symbols that are positive and symbols that are negative. I usually describe positive symbols as conveying hope or support, while negative symbols suggest obstruction or destruction. Although these descriptors may sound simple, my colleagues and I have found that they serve our students well. Every story that has a problem has symbols of obstruction or destruction, and nearly all stories, if not every story that gets resolved, has at least one symbol of hope and support. This is true whether the story is fiction or nonfiction.

Visual texts can have these symbols, too. Jackson's writing at the beginning of this chapter is a perfect example of a student applying ideas of hope and obstruction to different texts. Through the scaffolding of AoC, Jackson was able to think about the components of the painting *Lake George* and the characters from A Series of Unfortunate Events symbolically and then grow these two works of art into metaphors that could help him reflect on his own life. Finally, by sharing these metaphors, Jackson was able to convey a great point (find the sunny spots) and help others perhaps reflect on their own lives.

Again, it's not only older students like Jackson who benefit from thinking about symbols. I recently had a conversation with a small group of second graders, of whom only about 10 percent were reading at grade level. We began by briefly discussing how and why the blank paper in the first illustration from *The Dot* (see Figure 1.2) could be a symbol of frustration for Vashti. We then thought of other books that had characters or objects that could be seen as symbols of frustration. In just minutes, our conversation jumped from the blank paper in *The Dot* (Reynolds 2003) to discussing how the squirrels symbolized frustration to the old man in *Those Darn Squirrels!* (Rubin and Salmieri 2008), how the pig Mercy Watson from *Mercy Watson Goes for a Ride* (DiCamillo 2006) was a symbol of frustration to Eugenia Lincoln, how Amelia Bedelia (*Amelia Bedelia*; Parish 1963) became a symbol of frustration to anyone she worked for, how drawing turned into a symbol of frustration for Ramon in *Ish* (Reynolds 2004), which led them to pink becoming a symbol of frustration for Pinkalicious *Purplicious* (Kann and Kann 2007), and which finally led them to discussing how Luisa's polka-dot boots became a negative symbol for her in *Weird!* (Frankel and Heaphy 2012). In addition, when I asked whether students had any symbols of frustration in their own lives, Scarlett mentioned her sister, Mustafa mentioned the groundhog that keeps eating his family's flowers in their backyard, and Max mentioned math sheets.

By having these striving second-grade students think about symbols of frustration, I was able to help them access multiple different texts, develop their thinking, and use their voices to express their ideas. I guided a conversation that was filled with text-to-text connections and a few text-to-self connections, too. Overall, they performed similar kinds of thinking to what Jackson exhibited at the end of fifth grade through his writing. Those kiddos are on their way!

Furthermore, frequent conversations like these will help students engage with books that they'll read in the future as well as make it more likely that symbolism can be incorporated into their own writing. As I mentioned in Chapter 1, understanding how stories work is essential for both comprehension and writing. Making connections (through symbols and moods) helps students to understand this idea.

HELPING STUDENTS TO USE THE ACCESS LENSES

Students often need support to use Access Lenses effectively. When I work with classes, small groups, or individual students, I use different phrasing, depending on the amount of scaffolding the students need. The following are examples of how I vary statements or questions when I work with different students. The examples range from modeling my own thinking regarding the lenses to leaving the door wide open for students to share their own, perhaps unique, use of the lenses. In general, the level of scaffolding reduces as I go through the list. (Although I mainly use the facial expressions lens here, the different phrasings can pretty much be used with each of the lenses):

I'm looking at the character's face, and I'm thinking that the character feels upset because I can see the character's mouth is frowning.

I'm looking at the character's face, and I am thinking that the character feels upset. Does anyone know why I'm thinking that?

I see that the artist/illustrator described/drew the character's facial expression. How does the character's facial expression help us to think about the way the character is feeling?

Can we learn anything by looking at the character's facial expression?

Does the way the author described the facial expression tell us anything about how the character is feeling right now?

Can we use the facial expression lens to help us think about this picture/section of text?

What lenses can we use to help us think about what we read/are looking at?

What other lenses can we use to think about this illustration/image/passage?

What did/do you notice, and what does it make you think?

These phrases are not meant to always be used word for word. For instance, if you are talking about a certain character, you may want to use their name. When you model your use of the lenses, you want to be as specific as possible so that all of your students know where you are looking and what you are thinking.

INTRODUCING STUDENTS TO THE ACCESS LENSES

The Access Lenses are tools that even very young students can use. However, like all tools, the Access Lenses aren't much use on their own. Just like a hammer isn't much use unless you're putting something together or taking something apart, the Access Lenses won't be much help unless they are used to deconstruct or construct some sort of a text. When I introduce students to the Access Lenses, I show them the sheet and briefly go over each lens. However, it's not until the students see the Access Lenses used with a text that they really start to see how to use them.

In Chapter 3, I'll introduce the next component of AoC, the Framework. I'll show how the Framework and the Access Lenses can be used together when engaging with a visual text, which will help you and your students learn to use the Access Lenses efficiently and purposefully.

CHAPTER 3

The Framework

In Chapter 2, I introduced the Access Lenses, a tool that helps to give you and your students initial access to texts of all kinds (see Figure 2.2). In this chapter, I will outline the next tool of the Art of Comprehension (AoC): the Framework.

The Framework provides a means for introducing and using the Access Lenses. It's a sort of map, both for classroom conversations and for when students are working in groups or independently. Having this map helps make their thinking and conversations productive, which allows classroom time to be used efficiently.

The Framework also helps students to progress from simpler conversations to sophisticated ones. The beginning steps are more concrete, making them highly accessible to a wide range of students, while the later steps are more abstract. Engaging successfully with the easier, early steps helps students to organize information within the text so that they can engage meaningfully with the later steps.

The Framework is made up of the following six steps:

1. List everything you see (decode)
2. Determine the mood, and support your thinking with textual evidence
3. Think about what is causing the mood
4. Determine a big idea, a topic, or a theme of the text
5. Think about symbols (and/or metaphors)
6. Make a text-to-text, text-to-world, or text-to-self connection

The Framework as a whole is a ladder to support student comprehension, where each step supports and guides students to take the following step and thus construct ever-increasing depth of meaning. The Framework, as with the other components of AoC, isn't designed to help students find *the* answer; rather, it is designed to help students *explore* texts, so that they can construct possible answers in a meaningful and efficient manner. It does this by gently nudging them first to notice the information that the artist or author has provided and then to synthesize it with their schema. This, then, drives meaningful conversations about what the text may say explicitly and implicitly and how it may impact or inform the students' own lives.

TIPS FOR INTRODUCING THE FRAMEWORK

When you first explore the Framework with your students, if they get stuck on one step or become mentally exhausted, I suggest that you take a break and resume the process later in the day or even on another day. Sometimes with kindergarteners (especially if it is early in the year), in the first lesson, I will have them list everything they see and maybe briefly discuss the mood with them (Steps 1 and 2). The next time we meet we'll repeat whatever we accomplished (to help all the students become familiar with the process and the thinking) and then move on to discuss what is causing the mood and perhaps discover a big idea of the texts (Steps 3 and 4).

This slower pace benefits many students because it provides several opportunities for them to join the classroom conversation with meaningful answers. Perhaps more than anyone, striving students need these opportunities. Answering questions with answers that make sense, that are based on information within the text, and that are understood by others are powerful ways to build their confidence, which is essential to learning.

When students can access the Core Four (texts, thinking, voice, conversations) and are positively involved early in the year, a foundation is established for sophisticated and meaningful work later in the year. As Joan Moser (2017) likes to say, "You have to go slow in order to go fast." Reviewing and revisiting the steps is a good way to do this.

THE IMPORTANCE OF STEP 1: LISTING EVERYTHING YOU SEE (DECODE)

Although Step 1 is in some ways the simplest step, it can still feel foreign to students who are new to looking at visual texts closely. So I'd like to explain the thinking behind this step, which will help you to see its importance, especially for your striving students.

As a reading teacher, you know your students need explicit instruction to improve their reading. This is also true for visual texts. Listing everything you see sounds so simple, and it is, but most students and other novice viewers need both to be explicitly told to do this and to be shown how to do it. Listing everything in a picture is how a visual text is decoded. It is equivalent to reading every word on a page or in a paragraph. To make meaning efficiently with a written text, students can't read just some of the words, they need to read (or hear) all of them. Similarly, by being told to name anything that they can put a finger on in an image, students are gathering all of the textural evidence that the illustrator or artist has provided. If they see it, then they can use it to inform and support their thinking.

The listing step also ensures that every child can become an active participant because it is a simple way to help all students enter into the text and join the conversation. Once students have gone through the listing process a few times, or even just once, and they understand that I am literally asking them to say "nose" or "hands" or "yellow," most of them can come up with at least one meaningful answer and participate in a discussion around what they see. The process of saying and deliberately pointing to everything that can be seen also engages English language learners and helps them build their English vocabulary.

After explaining that we want to name anything that we can put our finger on and after modeling the process a few times, I'll often call on my shyest or most fragile learners first to offer an answer. They can usually say something that makes sense, and I can celebrate their answer like crazy. Sometimes the ability to give a single correct response in a whole-class setting can be a springboard to help these striving students to feel like part of the group.

When students begin to do this step, it's common for them to say that they see "happiness" or "sadness." Although the picture may indeed show one of these moods, it's important that you redirect them to list the things that they can put their fingers on. They can't put their fingers on happiness. They can put their fingers on a smile. What they can put their fingers on is the text evidence that you want them to notice and use.

I almost always have students do Step 1 orally. Writing out an actual list is too slow and labor intensive for most students, even for proficient writers. The last thing I want to do is set up an insurmountable obstacle before we even begin.

Just as with decoding written texts, students will develop proficiency with this step over time, which means less time needs to be spent explicitly focusing on it. Many of my students can now do Step 1 in about twenty seconds with minimal or no prompting. Keep in mind, however, that if it's a highly detailed picture, even the best students might need more time to take in and process what they are noticing.

I suggest you give your students all the time they need to take ownership of this first step. Seeing all the information in illustrations and artworks is crucial in order for them to have meaningful discussions. I sometimes find that, if the conversation isn't going well, it is because students didn't spend enough energy on this crucial step. When this happens, we "reread" and revisit this first step more deliberately.

USING THE ACCESS LENSES AND THE FRAMEWORK TOGETHER

What does it look like when the Access Lenses and the Framework are woven together? We will explore this union using the second picture I share with students and teachers whenever I am introducing or presenting AoC. It's the first illustration from another Peter H. Reynolds book, *Ish* (2004; see Figure 3.1).

1. List Everything You See (Decode)

When students are exploring the first step of the Framework, the Access Lenses can help them think about where to look to find potentially meaningful information. In looking at Reynolds's illustration, students could use the following lens: *faces, bodies, colors, close together, alone,* and *no words* (see Chapter 2) to guide their search. Typical responses that my students give are listed in Table 3.1.

TABLE 3.1

THE FRAMEWORK: STEP 1	**List everything you see (decode)**
Potential Student Responses	One person, eyes, face, mouth, hair, body, arms, legs, feet, yellow, white, black, green, gray, table, flowers, vase, wall, floor, picture, doorway, pen, brush, jar, drawings, clothes
Relevant Access Lenses	Facial expressions, body language/action, color, close together, alone, no words

FIGURE 3.1
The opening illustration from the book Ish *by Peter H. Reynolds*

A goal of noticing at least twenty things is helpful. Sometimes when I work with students, I ask them to find five things and then five more and so on. Continuously challenging them to find more information helps them learn to look closely and, thus, to realize how much information can be found in even the simplest images. Students also enjoy this challenge, which becomes a game to many of them.

2. Determine the Mood and Support Your Thinking with Text Evidence

After students gather information from the text, the next step is to use that information to infer the mood or moods of the image using textual evidence to support their thinking. They are essentially looking for patterns within the text: mood has to be crafted, and often there will be more than one piece of evidence to show it.

The Access Lenses cue students on where to look for information as they try to determine or infer the mood. For the image from *Ish* (see Figure 3.1), the faces and bodies lenses allow students to identify the boy's happy expression and relaxed attitude. They can begin to label the mood as happy and calm. Then the colors lens could help them to see that the bright yellow also indicates contentment and pleasure, suggesting a pattern (see Table 3.2). The Access Lenses help students to understand which information is important and which information they can use to support their thinking.

TABLE 3.2

THE FRAMEWORK: STEP 2	Determine the mood and support your thinking with text evidence
Potential Student Responses	Happy, relaxed, joyful, engaged, calm, content I can tell because . . . He's smiling, the bright colors, his body looks relaxed, he's kicking his feet, no one is bothering him, he's by himself, he's drawing/painting, it's quiet
Relevant Access Lenses	Facial expressions, body language/action, colors, no words, close together/far apart, alone

When students first get accustomed to determining the mood they will often use a limited vocabulary. The words *happy* and *sad* tend to come up a lot. To build student vocabulary and make our conversations more thoughtful, interesting, and precise, I create charts similar to Figure 3.2. Charts like this not only help conversation, they can also provide a word bank for students to use in their own writing.

3. Determine What Is Causing the Mood

Again, students can use the Access Lenses to help them infer the causes of the moods they've noticed. In Figure 3.1, the action, big things, close together, and alone lenses allow students to see that the boy is drawing, that drawing is important to him (he's close to his drawings and they take up a lot of picture space), and that he is absorbed in what he's doing. Then students can make a connection between the solitary drawing and the boy's happy mood.

If students can determine the cause of the mood or moods or at least provide an explanation that makes sense based on the textual evidence (visual or written), they are clearly making meaning of the text before

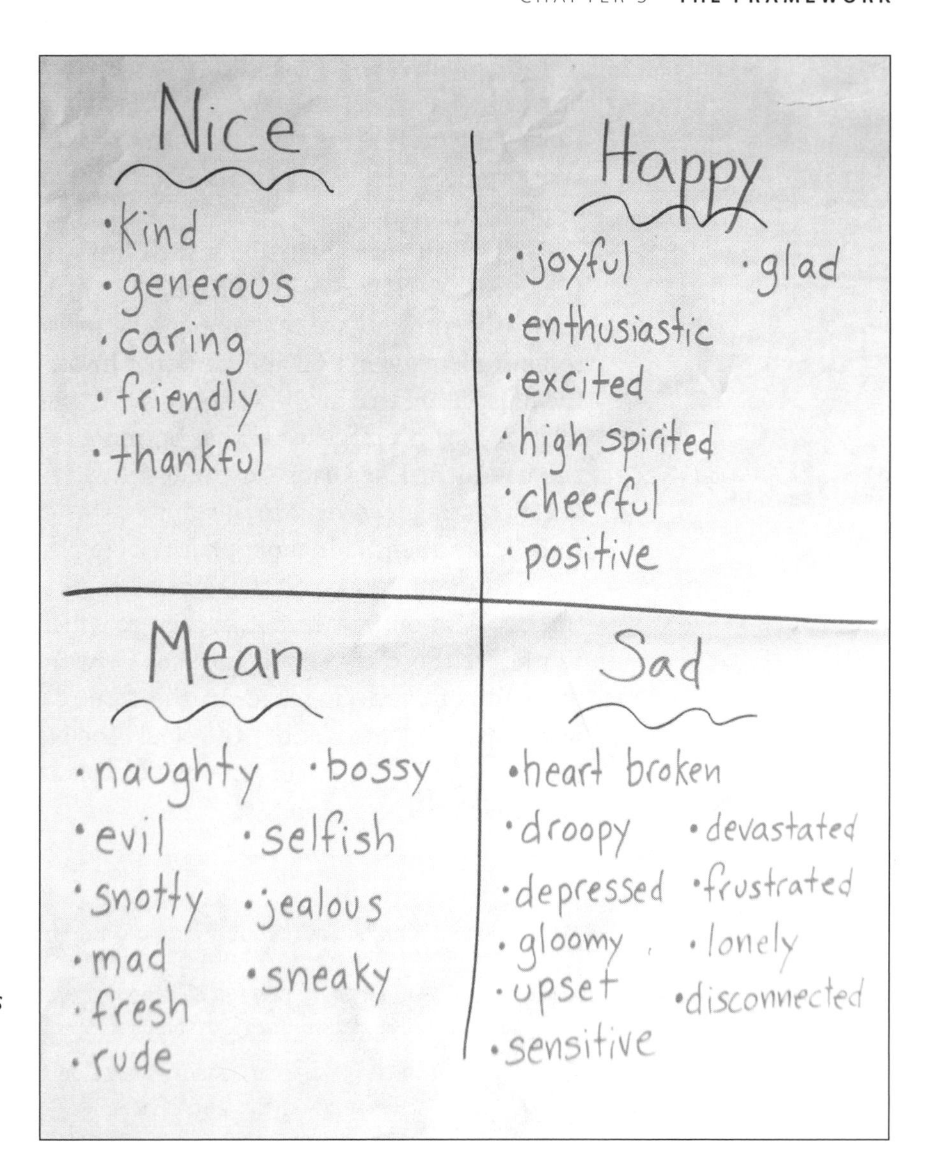

FIGURE 3.2
Creating a chart like this one from Mrs. Parella's fourth-grade class is a good way to help build student vocabulary.

them. This is true for both fictional and informational texts as long as they contain some sort of narrative, which most compelling writing does. Even nonfiction texts that inform students about a lion's day hunting in the African bush, describing travel conditions during Westward Expansion, or depicting the beginning of a sea turtle's life, will naturally include some storytelling elements. For students to understand these topics, they have to move beyond mere facts and grasp a sense of the moods in the writing and what causes them.

Often, this step is straightforward. Other times it can be difficult, because what is causing the mood isn't always explicitly stated. For some students, asking them to think about what is causing the mood is interpreted as giving permission for them to jump into the swamp of pure speculation.

Let's think once again about the illustration of Vashti from *The Dot* (Reynolds 2003; see Figure 1.2). Based on the evidence in the picture, most students will see that she is in some sort of negative mood. But some students won't be able to home in on particular information in the illustration to explain what might be causing that mood. Instead of relating Vashti's mood to school or, more specifically, recognizing that she has turned her back on the blank sheet of paper, they'll see this question as a green light to dive into a story that her frustration arises from space aliens kidnapping her cat. AoC can help these students because the Framework and the Access Lenses guide them to gather all of the information, organize it, recognize which details are key, and then synthesize those key details into coherent thinking that can be shared through common language. In the case of Vashti, the Access Lenses help these students identify the clock, the blank paper, and her turned back that can lead them to reasonable explanations about her bad mood (see Table 3.3).

TABLE 3.3

THE FRAMEWORK: STEP 3	**Think about what is causing the mood**
Potential Student Responses	The boy is happy because he is drawing/painting. I can tell he likes painting because he has a lot of drawings around him. The boy is happy because he is alone, not being bothered by anyone, doing something he likes.
Relevant Access Lenses	Action, big things (lots of drawings around him), alone, silence, no talking

When students do offer up a wild, long-winded tale of what's causing the mood that has very little grounding in the text, I ask them to support their thinking with evidence from the text. Often, I find that there may be one tiny bit of evidence that supports their theory, but since they aren't considering all of the evidence, there is no pattern in the text that backs up their idea. Part of what we want to do is to help students use all of the evidence within a text, not just some of it. So, this is a great opportunity to slow down and use the Access Lenses to help students focus on gathering all of the available textual evidence. You can discuss or model what that looks like.

With Step 3, keep in mind that sometimes what's causing the mood isn't apparent yet. Sometimes readers may know a character's mood and be able to support their thinking, but the book hasn't revealed the cause. In cases like this, students should be explicitly taught to consciously look for the information that reveals the causes as they read on.

4. Determine the Big Idea, Topic, or Theme of the Text

Big ideas or themes are often tied to the mood of a text, especially when viewing a single image. Because of this, once students determine a possible mood and what is causing it, they are able or close to being able to discuss the theme, big idea, or what the artist wants viewers to think about while transacting with the image. This is a good example of how the Framework steps build on the previous ones and supports students to take their next leap.

In Figure 3.1, once students have understood the boy's calm, happy mood while drawing alone, it's a relatively small jump to suggest that perhaps the artist wants us to think about how sometimes solitude can be contented and productive. In saying this, or something similar that captures this idea, they have moved from a mood to a big idea or theme (see Table 3.4).

TABLE 3.4

THE FRAMEWORK: STEP 4	Determine a big idea, topic, or theme
Potential Student Responses	Joy, happiness, peacefulness, quietness, calmness Or Sometimes it's wonderful doing something you love, peacefully by yourself. Being by yourself can be relaxing. Being alone can be joyful; it doesn't have to be lonely.
Relevant Access Lenses	Facial expression, body language/action, close together/far apart, alone, no talking, no sounds

When I first start discussing themes, I help students understand the difference between what the illustration shows and what it's about. In Figure 1.2, we see Vashti sitting alone in a room with her back turned toward a blank paper. That's what the image shows. However, what it is about, what the artist wants the viewers to think about, is frustration—or feeling stuck.

The experiences of your students discussing theme will largely determine what they will be able to do with this step. When viewing Figure 1.2 from *The Dot* (Reynolds 2003), less experienced students may only be able to come up with a single word to describe the picture, such as *frustrated, stuck, upset,* or *angry.* However, students who are more experienced may be able to say, "When we don't know what to do, it can make us feel frustrated." This type of response leans into ideas of universal theme and the lessons that books hold. Even if your students can't say it, you can, which guides them toward deeper, more sophisticated thinking. If my students are not generating any ideas or if I want to broaden their thinking, I might ask them, *Is this picture about sitting in a room alone or feeling frustrated? Which one sounds like a bigger idea? Which one sounds like a story?* Or, *What do you think the artist or writer wanted you to think about?* These questions help students not only to think more deeply about texts they read but also to think about idea generation and selection when it comes to their own writing. When students see that *The Dot* (Reynolds 2003) was crafted around a character who felt stuck and frustrated, they can think about times and reasons they or others have felt stuck or frustrated and then use these ideas in their own writing.

5. Think About Symbols or Metaphors

All artwork is symbolic. A picture of a tree isn't really a tree; just like the word *tree,* it is a symbol that represents an idea. That idea may include the idea of a tree, but it may just as easily represent the idea of strength or confidence. If it's a picture of a dead tree within a grove of living trees, it may symbolize the cycles of life or melancholy or isolation.

With a little experience of talking about symbols in texts, most students catch on to this type of thinking quickly. Although thinking of things as symbols is inherently abstract, humans are extremely good at it: young students will often draw the sun and rainbows in their drawings as a symbol of happiness. But beyond symbolic norms such as these, even young students are capable of thinking symbolically or metaphorically about objects, settings, actions, or characters. Think about how easily young children can associate objects and colors to people that they love. Almost as soon as my son could utter the word *Pa*, he would start up with a chorus of "Pa, Pa, Pa!" every time he saw a big gray van similar to his grandfather's. Clearly, he connected gray vans to his grandfather (not to mention the sound of "Pa" to a specific person).

As with the last step, determining the mood and what is causing the mood makes it easier for students to think about what characters, objects, settings, or activities within the text might represent or symbolize. Similarly, once students have some sense of big ideas or themes of the image, symbolic thinking becomes much more accessible. In the image from *Ish* (see Figure 3.1), understanding the happy mood and thinking about the theme of contented solitude makes it easier for students to view the boy's drawings as symbols of happiness or joy (see Table 3.5).

TABLE 3.5

THE FRAMEWORK: STEP 5	Think about symbols or metaphors
Potential Student Responses	Drawings/paintings can be a symbol of joy or happiness. Drawing/painting or creating can be a symbol of joy or happiness.
Relevant Access Lenses	Symbols, action, zoom in, big things (number of drawings)

Having students read symbolically is a wonderful way to help them think broadly and meaningfully about texts. Even nonfiction or informational topics can be viewed this way; think about the symbolic qualities of the lives of Thomas Edison (the importance of exploring ideas and persistence) or Rosa Parks (the struggle for equal rights). As much as we want students to learn the facts about these historic figures, we also want them to use what Edison and Parks symbolize to inform and inspire their own lives.

6. Make Connections

As I outlined in Chapter 1, making connections is a strategy that numerous professional books and articles for English language arts educators have discussed and described. It's one of the cornerstones of comprehension and there are lots of ways that students can make connections. Generally speaking, connections are often classified as:

Text-to-text
Text-to-world
Text-to-self

For students who are new to making connections, giving them specific elements of a text to make connections to can be helpful. Connections can be made to characters or figures from other books or movies, settings that are similar, a mood that has been crafted using the same Access Lenses, or symbols that have similar meanings.

Additionally, meaningful connections don't always have to be comparisons; they can also be contrasts. Sometimes talking about how characters, settings, moods, and symbols are different can be a great way to help students expand their understanding and demonstrate their comprehension and command over both of the texts being discussed. A text-to-text comparison of the image from *Ish* (see Figure 3.1) might contrast the bright colors with the muted colors of the image from *The Dot* (see Figure 1.2), which could demonstrate an understanding of the different moods of the characters as well as understanding of how they were crafted (see Table 3.6). Again, the early steps in the

TABLE 3.6

THE FRAMEWORK: STEP 6	**Make connections**
Potential Student Responses	This reminds me of the beginning of *Purplicious* when Pinkalicious is painting the sunset by herself and is happy. This is the opposite of *The Dot*. Ramon doesn't look upset at all. This reminds me of when I build with blocks in my room. I like it when nobody bothers me. This sort of looks like my cat, Oliver, when he lays in the sunlight. He always looks so calm and peaceful. It's one of his favorite things to do. He hates to be bothered. The other day I saw my sister reading in her chair by the window. She was happy just like Ramon because she loves to read.
Relevant Access Lenses	Body language/action, close together/far apart/alone, no sounds/no words, colors, symbols

Framework of determining moods and what is causing the mood and thinking about symbolism help students to take this last step of making connections.

MORE ON STEP 6: MAKING WEAK-LINK AND STRONG-LINK CONNECTIONS

When students make connections, it's important that they realize that not all connections are equal. I categorize connections into two kinds, weak-link and strong-link. Weak-link connections are superficial and don't move readers toward understanding. However, strong-link connections dig deep into the text and help readers build meaning around it.

Table 3.7 contains a few examples of weak-link and strong-link connections. Notice that the strong-link connections connect to the mood, while the weak-link connections do not. Teaching students to make connections through moods is an excellent way for them to learn to make their connections meaningful.

TABLE 3.7

Artwork	Weak-Link Connections	Strong-Link Connections
Picture of a sad boy curled up with a cat	"My uncle has a cat!"	"When I feel sad, I sometimes like to hold my stuffed animals. It makes me feel better."
Picture of a racing fire truck	"I like to go fast on my scooter!"	"When my brother got hurt, I ran as fast as I could to get my mom. We needed help."
Picture of Vashti sitting alone with her back turned	"I was alone in the classroom because I was the first one to school."	*Contrasting Connection* "When I am stuck on my homework, I'm always happy that my sister can help me so I don't feel like Vashti."

Another good way to make strong-link connections is through symbols. If, for example, we return to Vashti's blank paper (see Figure 1.2), and see it, her art class, the art room, or the act of drawing as symbols of frustration, it's relatively easy to make strong connections to other objects, to settings, or to activities in other texts or to our own lives that are also symbols of frustration.

AND EVEN MORE ON STEP 6: EXPANDING THE PURPOSE OF MAKING CONNECTIONS

Even though reading experts overwhelmingly support the practice of encouraging students to make meaningful connections to the texts they read, this strategy is actually underused. If we think about making connections as a reading comprehension strategy only, we severely limit its power, because the ability to make meaningful connections underlies so much other important work that we want students to do. Making connections as a cognitive activity goes far beyond comprehension.

For instance, making connections often comes up in the world of creativity and innovation. As Steve Jobs so simply put it, "Creativity is just connecting things." What Jobs meant is that the power of the ability to marry two seemingly unrelated ideas together is often what fuels creativity. A great example of this is when airbag makers connected the concept of airbags and origami; this connection enabled them to figure out how to fold airbags so that they could open with the most efficiency. Although the link may seem obvious now, someone originally had to span a giant gap to create this connection. Another example is this very book; I wouldn't be writing it if I hadn't started to see connections between best practices in English language arts instruction and viewing artworks. So why do I mention these things? Why is linking connection making and creativity important? Because from this stance, it's easy to argue that making connections not only impacts reading but also impacts writing.

Writing is an act of creativity and creativity requires connections. Creating a good simile or a high-quality metaphor requires making a connection between the thing being described and the thing being compared. Using a mentor text effectively requires a writer to make a connection, or many connections, between their manuscript and the author's manuscript. Developing a tone for a written piece and choosing a genre to present a topic requires the ability to see connections between content, craft, and audience. Word choice often requires the ability to connect words to moods accurately. Making connections is required to see patterns when students are reading but also for students to establish patterns for their readers when they are writing. All these are examples of why making connections is a wonderful strategy for students to use, whether they are making meaning from texts they read or creating meaning while crafting texts they write. (I'll develop this idea further in Chapter 6, when I explain how AoC can be used to support students when writing.)

Making connections also goes beyond reading comprehension because it also fosters engagement. In her blog post "What Current Brain Research Tells Us . . ." (2016), author Shaelynn Farnsworth states, "The brain hungers for meaning. Learners seek to make sense of information and recognize patterns, connections to prior knowledge and experiences and organize their learning around larger concepts." Recognizing patterns, connecting to prior knowledge and experiences, and organizing learning around larger concepts are all based on the ability to make connections. When we explicitly teach students to constantly make meaningful connections, we provide opportunities for them to create efficient links between content, craft, and their own lives, honoring their individual schemas and interests. Encouraging connections is an invitation for students to share all that they know and all that they love. It's an invitation to share who they are. What could be more engaging than that?

LAST THOUGHTS ON THE FRAMEWORK: IT'S A FLEXIBLE FRIEND, NOT A FIXED FORMAT

There is a useful phrase that I have heard often from English language arts educators: "Teach readers . . . not the book." It's important to remember that when introducing the Framework we are teaching the student, not the Framework. So although it is helpful to follow the steps in order when you first familiarize your students with the Framework, as they become more proficient at exploring visual and written texts using AoC, it's not always necessary or desirable to do this.

Using the Framework when reading a visual or written text is not meant to be like trudging up some institutional staircase. We are not trying to move students up through levels systematically with the goal of reaching the top floor. Using the Framework, paired with the Access Lenses, should be like hiking up meandering mountain trails that rise and fall as they follow the mountain's natural contours. Because each text is unique, each trail will be different, each start will be different, and each step could be different. Students who have internalized the Framework might sometimes start by determining the mood and then almost immediately make a strong-link connection. The Framework, like all the components of AoC, should serve the students to help them access texts, their thinking, their voice, and the classroom conversation and not become an end in itself.

The Framework steps are merely guidelines that have been very helpful to me in getting my students, even my reluctant and striving students, to dig deeper into texts and grow meaningful conversations around them. Ultimately, when hiking up the mountain, you as the guide will have to determine where to lead your students, when they need to stop and collect themselves, when to pause and take in the view, when to turn back, and when to move forward again. You'll also need to decide when your students are ready to explore and blaze new trails on their own.

So far, we have looked at two single illustrations from two different books by Peter H. Reynolds (2003, 2004) and explored how the Access Lenses and the Framework can be woven together to help students to make meaning out of them. I chose to use these images because they have been extremely effective when introducing students and other teachers to AoC. They are simple enough that all students can manage the information in them, yet sophisticated enough to spur engaging and thoughtful conversations even with older or soaring students.

However, I also chose these two images for another reason. The books that these two illustrations are from are great resources for introducing and exploring the third component of AoC, the Mood Structures. The Mood Structures are designed to support students when they are transacting with entire picture books, graphic novels, or other visual texts, such as movies or plays. The Mood Structures can also help students when they are reading written texts, such as chapter books, essays, and articles. I'll explain the Mood Structures next, in Chapter 4.

CHAPTER 4

The Mood Structures

If the Framework is like a map and the Access Lenses are like the tools, then the Mood Structures—the third component of the Art of Comprehension (AoC)—are like the weather reports, helping readers figure out what lies ahead. Like actual weather reports, they are not 100 percent perfect. But as with a weather report, just because they are not always 100 percent perfect doesn't mean they should be ignored. Trying to plan ahead helps you be prepared. It gets you ready. This principle can be applied to reading, too, because thinking about what's to come in texts, and getting ready for it, can help students to mix thinking with content, making them active readers (Harvey and Goudvis 2013).

In Chapters 1 and 3, we looked at two illustrations from books by Peter H. Reynolds: Figure 1.2 from *The Dot* (2003) and Figure 3.1 from *Ish* (2004). Through these two illustrations, we saw how the Framework and the Access Lenses can help students to think about and make meaning of parts of texts. In this chapter, I will show how the Mood Structures can help students consider how these parts fit together in an entire text.

The Access Lenses and the Framework can guide students to get their bearings when starting a story. Once they get their bearings, the Mood Structures give them a better sense of where the story might logically go. This helps readers do many things that are valuable for comprehension and engagement such as making strong-link connections (see Chapter 3), making predictions, and identifying key moments. The anchor charts in Figure 4.1 depict the three different Mood Structures that I share with my students.

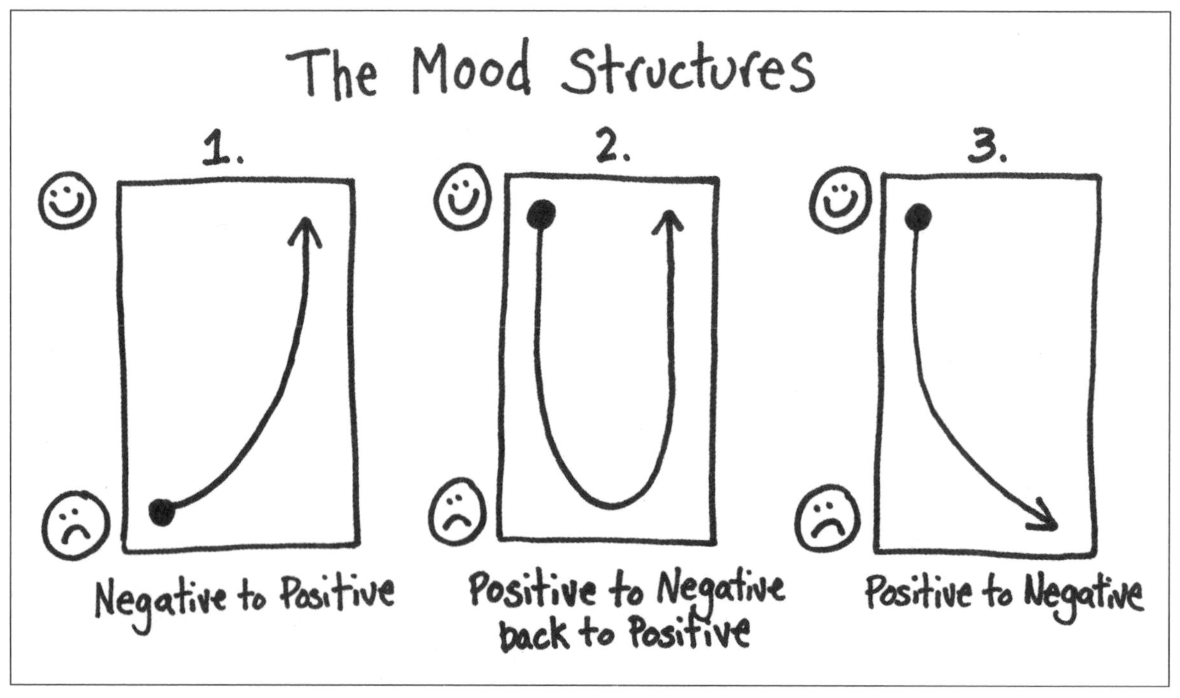

FIGURE 4.1
The Mood Structures provide visual representations of how texts can be constructed.

The Mood Structures are based on the idea of the story arc in that they provide a visual representation of how stories are constructed. However, because there are three different Mood Structures, instead of a single arc, they help students see specifically how different stories (and other texts) are actually presented from start to finish. The Mood Structures help students see how texts are crafted.

Because *The Dot* and *Ish* are not complicated stories, they are excellent for introducing the first two Mood Structures to students. Less complicated stories, just like less complicated weather conditions, are easier to predict and therefore line up better with the Mood Structures.

Let's start by returning to the first illustration from *The Dot* (Figure 4.2).

Before students can consider the Mood Structure of the story of *The Dot* (Reynolds 2003), they must determine its beginning mood: the mood with which the story starts. As I explained in Chapters 2 and 3, students can use the Framework and the Access Lenses to help them do this. Tables 4.1, 4.2, and 4.3 recap the deconstruction of the illustration using the first three steps of the Framework and the Access Lenses that we explored in the previous chapters.

FIGURE 4.2
The opening illustration from The Dot *by Peter H. Reynolds, depicting a negative mood*

TABLE 4.1

THE FRAMEWORK: STEP 1	List everything you see (decode)
Potential Student Responses	One person, eyebrow, mouth, hair, crossed arms, body, legs, fingers, shoes, a big room, seats, tables, tiles, whiteboard, clock, clock hands, doorway, greenish, blue, gray, pencils, whiteboard, blank paper
Relevant Access Lenses	Facial expression, body language/action, colors, alone, big/little, zoom in/zoom out/symbols

TABLE 4.2

THE FRAMEWORK: STEP 2	Determine the mood and support your thinking with text evidence
Potential Student Responses	Upset, angry, mad, disappointed, stuck, frustrated, annoyed I can tell that Vashti is upset because her eyebrow is slanted down and her body is turned around and slumping. Vashti's arms are crossed and her back is turned away from her paper. The colors are gloomy, and she is all alone. Vashti looks annoyed because she's not doing anything and she's not saying anything. She's just sitting there.
Relevant Access Lenses	Facial expression, body language, colors, far apart, alone, no words/silence, zoom in/zoom out

TABLE 4.3

THE FRAMEWORK: STEP 3	Think about what is causing the mood
Potential Student Responses	Vashti might be upset because she couldn't get an idea for her drawing. She might be upset because she doesn't know what to do and no one is helping her.
Relevant Access Lenses	Symbols, zoom in, far apart (from her paper, an idea and help), alone, silence

MAKING PREDICTIONS THROUGH THE MOOD STRUCTURES

Once students determine a beginning mood using the textual evidence, they can begin to think about the Mood Structures. Figure 4.2 depicts someone who is feeling upset, annoyed, frustrated, lonely, and so on. What is important is that students use textual evidence to determine that the character, Vashti, is in some sort of negative mood. Since this story starts off negative, the first Mood Structure is the best match.

Once students determine a mood and have a Mood Structure in mind they can begin to predict how the mood will change and what might cause the mood to change. The students' predictions may not be correct, but through their awareness of mood and Mood Structures they can develop a consistent and concrete way of thinking about how stories work. Thinking about Mood Structures, gets students actively looking for a change in mood, which often indicates a key moment or idea in both fictional and informational texts.

There are two kinds of predictions that students can make: general and specific. An example of a general prediction would be "I think Vashti is going to be happy by the end of the book." As simple as this prediction is, it's still a good prediction, especially for students who are new to thinking about moods and Mood Structures and are just starting to transact with books. It demonstrates that the student is thinking ahead and has an understanding of how stories generally work.

A specific prediction not only addresses expected future changes in the mood, as a general prediction does, but also considers what may cause those changes, usually by considering what has caused the beginning mood. An example of a specific prediction would be, "I think Vashti is going to be happy at the end because I think she is going to get an idea for her artwork." The more students think about the Mood Structures and what causes the moods in stories, the more likely it is that they will be able to make viable specific predictions based on the textual evidence presented by illustrators and authors.

By the end of the book, Vashti's mood has indeed changed from negative to positive, as students usually predict. Figure 4.3 is a picture from later in *The Dot* that depicts this mood change.

In this illustration, not only has the mood changed, but every Access Lens that was used in the beginning of the book to show the negative mood has flipped (or as my colleague Danielle Parella likes to say, "swung") to show the new, positive mood. Students can use the

FIGURE 4.3
An illustration depicting a positive mood near the end of The Dot

Framework and the Access Lenses to home in on this information. Table 4.4 shows how the Access Lenses can help students see the mood swing more clearly.

If you explore *The Dot* with your students, you'll witness these lenses slowly start to flip. When Vashti's teacher talks to her across several pages, readers can see Vashti gradually turn to face her blank page and begin to mark it up. Becoming sensitive to these subtle shifts helps students to track the development of characters or topics and gets them ready for the key moments when the mood changes.

Let's now revisit the book *Ish* (Reynolds 2004), which is a good example of the second Mood Structure: positive to negative and back to positive.

In Chapter 3, we looked at the first illustration, which shows Ramon joyfully drawing without distraction (see Figure 4.4). Using the Access Lenses, we were able to answer three powerful questions that get readers right into the heart of any narrative. These three questions are essentially Steps 2 and 3 from the Framework. I think of them as the mini-Framework. They are:

1. What's the mood?
2. How do you know the mood?
3. What's causing the mood?

Again, once a beginning mood has been determined, readers can think about the Mood Structures. In this case, we have a positive mood. As I showed in Chapter 3, the textual evidence supports this

TABLE 4.4

The Access Lens	First Illustration (Negative Mood)	Later Illustration (Positive Mood)
Facial expression	Frowning Furrowed brow	Smiling
Body language	Slumped, turned around, arms crossed	Standing straight, clutching paper, facing artwork
Colors	Darkish, gloomy, monochromatic	Bright, varied
Close together/far apart	Far from artwork and people	Close to artwork and people
Alone	Alone	Not alone
Silence/sounds or words	Silence	Talking
Big and little things	Grumpiness is big Little work (nothing done)	Happiness is big Work is plentiful and huge
Zoom in/zoom out	Zoom in on the blank paper	Zoom out on all of the artwork
Symbols	Blank paper is a symbol of frustration	Artwork is a symbol of joy and happiness

and suggests that drawing by himself is the root cause of Ramon's happiness. After my students determine the mood of this picture, I ask them, "So, do you think the story is going to go 'Ramon was happy, happy, happy, the end?'" After hearing a chorus of "No!" I ask them to predict what the Mood Structure will be. Many students, even from my youngest classes, usually will predict that the mood will turn negative. After drawing a line to indicate the mood going down, I ask them, "Do you think this is how the story will end? Ramon's life will be terrible ever after—the end?" After hearing another chorus of "No!" I ask the students to predict what the mood will be at the end. At this point, almost all of the students predict that the story will finish up happy. Then I ask, "Why does this prediction makes sense?" to which the students basically respond, "Because that is how most stories end!"

FIGURE 4.4
The opening illustration from the book Ish *by Peter H. Reynolds depicting a positive mood*

Once students determine the mood and what is causing the mood, and once they have a Mood Structure in mind, they are in a good position to make specific predictions. For instance, in the picture of Vashti (Figure 4.2), the reader doesn't know whether her paper is empty because she doesn't have any ideas, because she misunderstood the directions, or because the project is too hard. But we do know she is upset because her paper is empty, and therefore, a strong prediction, at this point, will be the use of the blank paper as a springboard to imagine how her mood could change. Maybe someone will help her, or maybe she will get an idea. Predictions don't have to be perfect, but they do have to be logical, based on the evidence in the story. Determining the mood, determining the causes of the mood, and thinking about Mood Structures help students to make logical predictions based on the information provided by the artist or author.

MAKING CONNECTIONS THROUGH THE MOOD STRUCTURES

When students recognize a Mood Structure and use it to make a prediction, they are well positioned to make connections because any story that starts out negative usually is going to end positively. As students are exposed to more stories and as they recognize Mood Structures within them, they will be able to see similarities between texts and make more strong-link connections. These strong-link connections, based on an understanding of how stories work, help students to establish solid mental representations of story structures (and eventually chapter structures). These representations help students manage and contextualize information as they read, which helps them grow their ideas and make meaning as they navigate their way through texts.

A SLIGHT DETOUR: AoC AND THE IMPORTANCE OF MENTAL REPRESENTATIONS

In their book, *Peak: Secrets from the New Science of Expertise*, Anders Ericsson and Robert Pool define a mental representation as "a mental structure that corresponds to an object, an idea, a collection of information, or anything else, concrete or abstract, that the brain is thinking about" (2016, 58). They explain that we all use mental representations all of the time and that these mental representations "make it possible to process large amounts of information quickly despite the limitations of short term memory" (61). They go on to explain that "experts" have formed many highly developed and specialized mental representations "which in turn make possible the incredible memory, pattern recognition, problem solving, and other sorts of advanced abilities to excel in their particular specialties" (63). If we want to help our students to become expert meaning-makers of texts, then it makes sense that we help them develop accurate mental representations around texts. This is what AoC does.

The three components of AoC—the Access Lenses, the Framework, and the Mood Structures—help students develop three mental representations that they can use to make meaning. The Access Lenses help students establish a mental representation to find the information that they need within texts. The Framework helps students establish a mental representation to learn how to take the information they have found, synthesize it, and grow meaningful ideas with it. And the Mood

Structures help students to form a mental representation that helps students understand how texts can be structured. Together, these three tools help students to form more highly detailed mental representations of how texts work and how meaning gets made from them. These mental models help students make meaning while they read and put them on a path toward expertise. As Ericsson and Pool point out, "In pretty much every area, a hallmark of expert performance is the ability to see patterns in a collection of things that would seem random or confusing to people with less well developed mental representations" (2016, 63). Expert performance in reading comprehension seems to be no different. Ericsson and Pool conclude that "the key benefit of mental representations lies in how they help us deal with information: understanding and interpreting it, holding it in memory, organizing it, analyzing it and making decisions with it" (66). These are all things that our readers need to do. The components of AoC provide a means to help students to do this important work.

GETTING BACK TO THE MOOD STRUCTURES

Let's continue with *Ish* (Reynolds 2004) and look at an illustration from the middle of the book that depicts a much more negative mood, mirroring the second Mood Structure (see Figure 4.5, page 56).

As with previous illustrations, students can use the Framework and the Access Lenses to break this illustration down (see Tables 4.5—4.10).

Finally, let's look at a third illustration from *Ish* (Reynolds 2004), one that appears toward the end of the book and depicts a return to a more positive, joyous mood (see Figure 4.6, page 57).

Instead of deconstructing this image using the previous model, I'd like to introduce a graphic organizer, based on the Access Lenses, that has been helpful to students (see Figure 4.7, page 58). I sometimes create this graphic organizer as a large anchor chart; or, for students who can write, I give them one to be filled in independently or with partners. It is a good way to get students to look for and organize the textual evidence that can inform their thinking.

(Text continues on page 59)

TABLE 4.5

THE FRAMEWORK: STEP 1	List everything you see (decode)
Potential Student Responses	Eyebrow, arm, lines, red, gray, crumbled paper, flowers, table, chair
Relevant Access Lenses	Facial expression, action, color, symbol, zoom in

TABLE 4.6

THE FRAMEWORK: STEP 2	Determine the mood and support your thinking with text evidence
Potential Student Responses	Frustrated, angry, mad His face looks angry because of his eyebrow. Throwing the paper and knocking over the flowers makes him look angry, too. The red in the background could symbolize anger. And the color isn't in the flowers anymore. It's like his happiness is gone, destroyed. He's no longer close to his artwork. Being close used to make him happy.
Relevant Access Lenses	Facial expression, action, color, far apart, alone, zoom in

TABLE 4.7

THE FRAMEWORK: STEP 3	Think about what is causing the mood
Potential Student Responses	He's frustrated about his drawing. (Prior to this page, Ramon's older brother, Leon, made fun of Ramon's drawing. Leon's words and laughter hurt Ramon's feelings.) Leon is the cause of Ramon's mood.
Relevant Access Lenses	Facial expressions, action, words, symbols, close together

FIGURE 4.5
An illustration depicting a negative mood from the middle of Ish

TABLE 4.8

THE FRAMEWORK: STEP 4	Determine a big idea, topic, or theme
Potential Student Responses	Frustration, anger
Relevant Access Lenses	Facial expression, action, color, symbols

TABLE 4.9

THE FRAMEWORK: STEP 5	Think about symbols or metaphors
Potential Student Responses	I think the artist wanted us to think about feeling frustrated or angry. I think the flowers exploding can be a symbol of how Ramon feels, like he wants to explode. The flowers losing all of their color is like Ramon losing all of his joy.
Relevant Access Lenses	Facial expressions, action, colors

FIGURE 4.6
An illustration depicting a positive mood near the end of Ish

TABLE 4.10

THE FRAMEWORK: STEP 6	Make connections
Potential Student Responses	This reminds me of Vashti at the beginning of *The Dot*. I'm surprised she didn't crumple up her paper. This reminds me of the first time I struck out. I threw my helmet and slammed down my bat. Ramon looks like my little sister when she is having a tantrum. She throws everything!
Relevant Access Lenses	Facial expressions, action

Name: ______________________

Mood/Change in Mood: Joyful

We can use the Access Lenses to help us think about and discuss the moods and text evidence in stories.

Colors	Bodies/ Action	Faces
Bright Cheerful Sunny Warm	laying on belly legs kicking painting	Smiling
Close Together Far Apart •close to artwork •far from being bothered •far from concern Alone alone	Words/ No Words Quiet no talking peaceful Sounds/ No Sounds	Big Things stacks of drawings Concentration Little Things
Zoom in smile drawing squiggles Quiet, empty room Zoom Out	Symbol/Mood Drawing is happiness Drawing is joy	Connections Beginning of Purplicious Building with legos Reading

Determining moods, what's causing the mood and how and why these moods change helps us to think about and discuss stories more deeply.

FIGURE 4.7
Using this graphic organizer (see Appendix A) or creating an anchor chart based on the Access Lenses can help students organize textual evidence.

RETELLING AND SUMMARIZING THROUGH THE MOOD STRUCTURES

The Mood Structures also provide an easy format to help students learn to retell or summarize fictional or informational stories that they have read. Once students learn and recognize the Mood Structures, they can act as a cue to help students know what information they need to include in their retell or summary. For instance, if the story matches the first Mood Structure, students may say something like

1. In the beginning of the story the main character(s) felt ______________ because . . .
2. But by the end of the story the main character(s) felt ______________ because . . .

And if the story follows the second Mood Structure, students may say something like

1. In the beginning of the story the main character(s) felt ______________ because . . .
2. Then in the middle of the story the main character(s) felt ______________ because . . .
3. But by the end of the story the main character(s) felt ______________ because . . .

Obviously, complicated stories may require more than two or three sentences to provide a sufficient summary but having a clear mental representation of how stories generally work will help many students, especially striving students, get started. These representations will also help students develop awareness of two of the most important aspects of fictional and informational stories: *how* character's change and *why* they change.

To summarize, after students learn these Mood Structures, they will have two clear and concrete ways of thinking about how texts unfold, and they'll recognize them in all kinds of texts. This, in turn, will help them to make predictions, to identify key moments, to make meaningful strong-link connections, and to summarize or retell.

USING MOOD STRUCTURES TO THINK ABOUT THEME, BIG IDEAS, AND LESSONS

Themes, big ideas, and lessons are found among moods. In texts that present more than one mood, how and why moods change gets at the heart of the story. If students can explain how and why the moods changed from the beginning to the end of a story, they are right on the cusp of discussing the possible themes, big ideas, or lessons of that story.

The Dot (Reynolds 2003) is basically a story that starts off with a young girl, Vashti, who doesn't like to draw, but by the end of the book, Vashti winds up really enjoying making art. So why did her mood change? Well, let's look at two of the reasons and see how these reasons can help students think about some bigger meanings of this story.

One reason is that Vashti's teacher kindly nudges her to get started by encouraging her to make a simple mark. This initial nudge eventually led to a change in mood for Vashti. Hence, one of the themes we can take away is *sometimes when we feel stuck or frustrated, we all can use a little support or help*. Another reason Vashti's mood changed is that, once she got started, she realized that she actually could do lots of great work. This mood change illustrates the theme: *you never know what will happen until you try.*

Essentially, in both of these examples, *why* the mood changes encapsulates a lesson, a big idea, or a theme within the story. And *how* the mood changes provides the evidence to support the thinking behind these lessons, big ideas, or themes. Once Vashti got the support she needed, she went from feeling stuck and frustrated to feeling confident and creative. Or, once Vashti started working, she began to see endless possibility and went from feeling like an incapable student to a joyful creator. If students are trying to explain how this story illustrates either of these themes, having a handle on how and why the mood changed will make it much easier for them to do so.

MOOD STRUCTURE FREQUENCY

Nearly every story has at least one Mood Structure within it. However, the first two Mood Structures are by far the most common since the vast majority of texts that you and your students encounter will end on a positive note. The third Mood Structure, positive to negative, is relatively rare in texts for younger readers, and I usually think of this Mood Structure in relation to works crafted for adults, such as Shakespeare's *Romeo and Juliet* (2011) or Arthur Miller's *Death of a Salesman* (1998). However, there are some books for younger audiences that do have this Mood Structure within them. The picture book *Each Kindness* (Woodson and Lewis 2012) ends with the main character feeling regret. The chapter books *Stone Fox* (Gardiner 1980) and *Bridge to Terabithia* (Paterson 1977) also contain this Mood Structure. As students watch sophisticated movies and shows, they are more likely to see this Mood Structure showing up more frequently.

GOING ON A MOOD WALK

One of my favorite ways to help students think about moods within stories is by going on a mood walk. Mood walks help students to become more aware of moods, textual evidence, key moments (changes in mood), and Mood Structures. The concept is similar to a picture walk, except that students focus on the mood. As we walk through the picture book, students look at the illustrations only and answer two questions: *What's the mood?* and *How do you know?* This allows them to identify a mood in the beginning of the story and then watch to see how and when it changes throughout the book. Students can partner up for this work so that they can share their thinking. After the partner work is complete, I give several students an opportunity to share their ideas with the whole group.

After our mood walk, we go back and read the written text of the story. Students are usually excited to learn more details provided by the written text so they can find out exactly what caused the moods and changes in the moods that they saw in the pictures. Paying close attention to the moods and how they change in the illustrations of the text can help every student become more engaged and active in their reading of the whole text, written and visual. Because stories are told through moods, when students enter a text through mood, they will be dancing with the soul of the story.

SINGLE MOODS

Not all texts have a Mood Structure. Some texts (as well as some scenes or chapters) consist of a single mood; many paintings, poems, songs, articles, and essays are apt to be crafted in this way. The Mood Structures, as with the Access Lenses, are tools to be used when they are appropriate. As readers, students shouldn't be trying to drive a screw with a hammer: they should learn to use the right tool for the job.

TRUST THE JOURNEY

Over the course of the years since I started using AoC, I've had dozens of conversations with students and colleagues about artworks and books, such as *The Dot* and *Ish*. One of the things I have found to be both amazing and inspiring is how varied these conversations can be. I am often blown away by what a student or colleague says about one of these works with which I am so familiar. By sharing their thoughts, by sharing themselves, they gift new ways of seeing, thinking, and knowing to everyone involved in the conversation. This is what great conversations about art do, regardless of the art form.

Every time I start a conversation, it's like a start of a journey. And although the destination may be somewhat familiar, how we get there and the discoveries we make along the way often fill me with wonder. When you work with AoC, let your students explore pictures and texts for as long as they are engaged. Be open to letting questions hang to give your students plenty of time to think. I've had groups, younger and older, work with a single illustration for more than twenty minutes. It is amazing what can happen when we provide space for individual voices to rise up and be heard. It's amazing what can happen when students share and grow their thinking. Trust the journey, trust the art, trust the book, and trust your students. They all have gifts to give. Some students simply need a bit more time to learn how to give them.

So far, we have looked at how the Framework, the Access Lenses, and the Mood Structures can be applied to visual texts, such as paintings and illustrations. In Chapter 5, we'll move away from visual texts and explore how the components of AoC can be applied to written texts. As you read the next chapter, keep in mind that, although the type of text changes, the conversation doesn't change much. You and your students will still use the Framework, the Access Lenses, and the Mood Structures to enter into the written text, think about it meaningfully, and talk about it purposefully.

CHAPTER 5

Reading Written Texts Through AoC

The **idea that** pictures and writing are both forms of texts has been around for centuries. Leonardo da Vinci famously declared, "Painting is poetry that is seen rather than felt and poetry is painting that is felt rather than seen." Even prior to Leonardo's statement, the Greek philosopher Plutarch, who lived from AD 46 to AD 120 is quoted as stating, "Painting is silent poetry and poetry is painting that speaks." Yet, despite these centuries-old declarations, students are often taught substantially different ways to comprehend these two forms of texts. The Art of Comprehension (AoC) challenges this practice and provides a single approach that can be used to engage with nearly any form of text.

The same three tools—the Access Lenses, the Framework, and the Mood Structures—that students learn to use by working with highly manageable visual texts can be used to help construct meaning in other types of texts, including written ones. This provides remarkable consistency for students across grades and subjects and helps them tackle various forms of text with confidence and purpose.

To get a clearer picture of how this works, use the three components of the AoC with the following brief passage. Even when exploring a mere thirty-two words, AoC can help readers to think deeply about the passage and to grow ideas around it, which helps students with meaning-making. The passage is from the Goosebumps book *Dr. Maniac Will See You Now*, written by R. L. Stine (2013, 84).

> Bree stayed close behind us. I knew she was really worried about her parents. Her face was pale, her expression grim. She didn't bother to fix her hair. She didn't say a word.

1. List everything you see (decode)

As I detailed in Chapter 3, the first step is always to decode. Visual texts and written texts both need to be decoded before the work of meaning-making can begin. However, a visual text and a written text are decoded differently. With visual texts, the teacher, the students, or some combination of the two *lists everything they see*. With written texts, the teacher, the students, or some combination of the two *reads every word*. But other than *how* the text is decoded, the rest of the work is the same.

2. Determine the mood and support your thinking with text evidence

In this passage, Stine uses direct characterization to tell the reader that the mood is worried. The line "I knew she was really worried" is the evidence to support this. However, Stine also provides more text evidence by describing her facial expressions, her color, her position, her silence, and her inaction (see Table 5.1). Essentially, Stine's words create a picture that illustrates the mood. Therefore, students can use the Access Lenses to pull information out of text the same as when they explore visual texts.

3. Think about what is causing the mood

Although we would need more information to determine the exact cause of Bree's worry, we know from the text that her worry is related to her parents ("I knew she was really worried about her parents"). So now students can answer the three questions that make up the mini-Framework:

What's the mood?
How do you know what it is?
What's causing the mood?

And as I said in Chapter 4, when they can answer these three questions, students are well positioned to think about and discuss the text meaningfully and deeply.

TABLE 5.1

Text Evidence Showing the Worried Mood	Relevant Access Lenses
Bree stayed close behind us.	Close together
Her face was pale . . .	Color
. . . her expression grim.	Facial expression
She didn't bother to fix her hair.	Action (in this case, inaction)
She didn't say a word.	No words, silence

4. Determine a big idea, a topic, or a theme of the text

Just as with visual texts, the mood is closely related to the big idea or theme of the text. The big idea of the Stine (2013) paragraph is that Bree feels worried. Stine wants his readers to think about this as they read. That's why it's in the story. Awareness of this mood helps readers enter into the meaning of this moment, which helps them get ready for a key future moment in the story—when Bree's mood will change.

5. Think about symbols (or metaphors)

Characters, objects, events, or settings that cause or influence a mood can be thought of symbolically. Bree is worried about her parents; to put it another way, her parents (or events related to her parents) are causing her worried mood. To understand why Bree would be worried about her parents, students might think about what parents symbolize: support, stability, love, and comfort. If something happens to Bree's parents, she may lose all of this. When readers understand the symbolic nature of character, objects, events, and settings, it helps them also to understand the reason for the characters' or subjects' mood, thus helping them to comprehend the whole text.

Although it may seem insignificant or even unnecessary to discuss the symbolic nature of Bree's parents in a book from the Goosebumps series, conversations about the symbolism of simpler books prepare students to work with literary works in which the symbolic nature of characters, objects, events, and settings is crucial to understanding larger meanings.

6. Make a connection

Once students have determined the mood of the text and thought about symbols that appear in it, they have access points for making strong-link connections. (If necessary, see Chapter 3 for details about what makes a strong-link connection.) Students might think of a time that they themselves or a character felt worried about something; or they might reflect on who symbolizes support, stability, love, or comfort either in their own lives or in another story. Making strong-link connections helps students to develop empathy for the characters and allows them to use the text to reflect on and comprehend their own lives. Students can make additional strong-link connections by thinking of other stories that portrayed negative moods and then use that knowledge along with the Mood Structures to predict what may happen to change Bree's mood.

Good writers like Stine continually create pictures with words that work to reveal the mood, which is why students can use AoC when reading as they would if they were viewing an illustration or other visual artwork. The information being delivered is the same; however, the delivery system is different.

Short passages such as Stine's is a great way to introduce students to using the Framework and the Access Lenses with written text. Short texts make the work more manageable for many students, which creates opportunities for students to find success and confidently demonstrate their meaning-making skills from the start. It's analogous to introducing the visual application of AoC using a single illustration, as outlined in Chapter 1. Completing some of these steps with a brief paragraph may seem simplistic, but it provides an often necessary scaffold for learners to help them to be able to do this work with longer texts, where more information needs to be processed and managed. When AoC is first used with written texts, be aware of the different levels of support that students might need to transfer the tools from visual texts. The questions from the end of Chapter 2 may be helpful to support this transfer.

Work with these paragraphs can be done through whole-group instruction, in small groups, in pairs, or individually. Sometimes, the teachers that I work with or I pick a short passage from the current or a favorite read-aloud. Students love to explore AoC using the texts they already know and enjoy. Sometimes, we even pick two passages that demonstrate a change in mood, which help students to become more aware of these changes. This brings the Mood Structures into play.

THE MOOD STRUCTURES AND WRITTEN TEXT

When I introduced the Mood Structures in Chapter 4, I shared an illustration from the beginning of *The Dot* (Reynolds 2003; see Figure 4.2) and then an illustration toward the end of the book (see Figure 4.3). I'll do the same now, except, instead of illustrations, I want to share a couple of short passages of text from *The Lemonade War* by Jacqueline Davies (2007), one from the beginning and one nearer the end.

Through these two passages, I'll continue to examine how authors craft moods to drive their stories and how the Framework and the Access Lenses can help students think about and discuss written texts. You will also see that, as in *The Dot* (Reynolds 2003) and in *Ish* (Reynolds 2004), the mood flips between the two passages and that (as I showed with the visual examples in Chapter 4) the flip can be identified using the Access Lenses. The clear change in mood also creates the Mood Structure of the text.

The first passage in *The Lemonade War* is from early in Chapter 1, which is entitled, "Slump." Even from the chapter's title, we get a clear indication that the chapter will establish a negative mood. Sure enough, among other negative things, Davies describes a boy, Evan, in self-imposed isolation, avoiding his sister, and a heat wave described as "giving-up kind of weather" (2007, 3).

Before you read the passage, I suggest that you review the Access Lenses and the Framework. Then get ready to use them to ask yourself, *What's the mood, and what evidence supports my thinking?* Even in the first sentence, readers can use several of the Access Lenses to zero in on information that gives an idea of how the character is feeling—in other words his mood (Table 5.2).

> Hopefully she wouldn't ask him why he was hiding in the dark basement. And hopefully Jessie wouldn't be in the kitchen at all. He'd been avoiding her for two days now, and it was getting harder by the minute. The house just wasn't that big.

Now let's look at how the mood flips near the very end of the story, following the Mood Structure of negative to positive (Table 5.3). Davies writes:

> "Not a bad seat," said Mrs. Treski, patting the step. "Enjoy."
> For twenty minutes, the night sky was alive with wagon

TABLE 5.2

Text	Relevant Access Lens	Inference/Mood/Meaning
Hopefully she wouldn't ask him . . .	Words or no words	Doesn't want to talk about it
. . . hiding in the dark basement	Color/alone	Avoidance/gloomy
And hopefully Jessie wouldn't be in the kitchen at all	Far apart	Doesn't want to see her/ avoidance
He'd been avoiding her for two days . . .	Far apart/big thing	Avoidance. It's a big deal because two days is a long time.
. . . getting harder by the minute.	Close together	He knows he's going to have to deal with the problem soon.
The house just wasn't that big.	Big and little things	It's a big problem and it's going to have to be addressed soon.

> wheels, party colored dahlias and whistling glitter palms. Evan, Jessie and Mrs. Treski sat [together on the step] watching, silent but for the occasional "Oohhh" and "Aahhh" that seemed to escape from their lips like hissing air from an overblown tire. (2007, 171)

If students tracked and recorded these moods across the text, similarly to Tables 5.2 and 5.3, and then compared their notes, they could clearly see that the beginning mood of the story flips by the end. In the beginning, Evan was alone in the dark basement, not wanting to talk. By the end of the story, Evan is sitting close to his mom and sister, they are talking, and the night sky is filled with bright, celebratory color.

From this perspective, it's fairly easy to make a strong-link connection to *The Dot* (Reynolds 2003). In the beginning of *The Dot*, Vashti, similarly to Evan, was in a negative state, alone, not talking to anyone, and was surrounded by darkish colors. By the end of the story, Vashti, again similarly to Evan, was with other people and surrounded by her colorful artworks that are like the "party colored" fireworks. The Mood Structures in both stories goes from negative to positive. Tracking the moods and how and why they change over the course of the text is a

TABLE 5.3

Text	Relevant Access Lens	Inference/Mood/Meaning
"Not a bad seat . . . Enjoy"	Words	The characters are now talking to each other kindly.
. . . patting the step.	Action/close together	Invitation to sit: they are no longer far apart physically or emotionally.
. . . the night sky was alive . . . party colored dahlias . . . glitter palms	Color/symbol	The mood is joyful and celebratory.
. . . whistling . . .	Sound, symbol	Whistling can be a happy, joyful sound.
. . . Sat watching . . .	Close together	They are content and comfortable.
. . . silent. . .	No words	They are content and comfortable.
"Oohhh" and "Aahhh"	Sound	Enjoyment.
. . . like hissing air from an overblown tire.	Sound, big and little things, symbols	The hissing is like a breath out. The tension is gone and the problem, like the tire, which had stretched beyond capacity, has shrunk and wilted to nothing.

great way for students to see how individuals or characters develop and how different parts of the text relate. At first, students who are new to AoC might need to be prompted to do this kind of work, but as they become more familiar and confident with the tools, they will do this work more independently and automatically.

Another example of the mood flipping from the beginning of the story to the end of the story comes from Kate DiCamillo in *The Tiger Rising* (2001), which was selected as a National Book Award Finalist in 2001. Again, as you read the passage from page 2 of the book, think about the Access Lenses. Which ones can be applied, and how can they help you and your students to think about the mood and how it's being crafted (Table 5.4)?

TABLE 5.4

Text	Relevant Access Lenses	Inference/Mood/Meaning
. . . looked like it might rain . . .	Color, symbols	Dreary, gloomy
. . . it had been raining everyday for almost two weeks.	Color, big things	Gloomy, two weeks is a long time to experience rain/gloom
The sky was gray . . .	Color	Gloomy
. . . and the air was thick and still.	Action, inaction	Suffocating, not moving/ uncomfortable
Fog was hugging the ground.	Action	Clinging relentlessly

> It was early morning and it looked like it might rain; it had been raining every day for almost two weeks. The sky was gray and the air thick and still. Fog was hugging the ground.

As you can see, DiCamillo's description and word choices have a negative tone. The passage as a whole comes across as dreary and oppressive. In this chapter, DiCamillo, just like Peter H. Reynolds with Vashti and Jacqueline Davies with Evan, also has her main character alone. By thinking through mood and using the Access Lenses, it's easy to make strong-link connections between these three texts.

If students look at the text evidence from the last page of *The Tiger Rising*, they will see how the mood has changed and how this change has been shown (Table 5.5).

> "See?" said Sistine in his dream. "I told you it was like fireworks."
> He woke up smiling, staring at the ceiling of the motel room.
> "Guess what?" his father called to him from outside.
> "What?" said Rob back.
> "There ain't a cloud in the sky," said his father, "that's what."
> Rob nodded. He lay in bed and watched the sun poke its way through his curtain. (DiCamillo 2001, 121)

TABLE 5.5

Text	Relevant Access Lens	Inference/Mood/Meaning
. . . it was like fireworks.	Color lens Action lens	Celebratory, exciting, cheerful
He woke up smiling . . .	Facial expression lens	Happy, content
There ain't a cloud in the sky.	Color lens	Perfect, beautiful
. . . watched the sun poke its way through the curtain.	Color lens	Bright, warm, positive, cheerful, relaxed

Although I used these four passages from *The Lemonade War* (Davies 2007) and *The Tiger Rising* (DiCamillo 2001) to illustrate the negative-to-positive Mood Structure, I don't mean to suggest that novels can always be represented using a single Mood Structure. In many novels, including children's literature and young adult novels, characters go through a wide range of emotions. They may feel despair or hope, loneliness or connectedness, anger or sadness or joy at any point within the story. This range of emotions, deliberately crafted by writers, creates the emotional roller coasters within stories that keep readers (or viewers) engaged and wanting more. This is what makes stories enjoyable.

In plays and movies, these mood shifts are often placed at the end of scenes to keep the audience in their seats. In television, the shifts often occur right before a commercial break, which gets viewers coming back after the commercials (at least when people watched commercials). In novels, these mood changes often occur at the beginning or end of chapters to keep readers turning pages. As I've said several times (but it bears repeating), students need to be aware of these big shifts in mood because they signify key moments within the story. If things are going wonderfully for the main character, students should be thinking, *This is too good to be true.* If things are going horribly, students should be thinking, *There has to be a symbol of hope or support showing up soon.*

E. B. White's classic *Charlotte's Web* (1952) is a great example of these kinds of mood changes. The first chapter starts off with the father, Mr. Arable, going to kill the runt from the litter of pigs born the night before. This establishes a negative mood. The chapter ends with the daughter, Fern, talking her father out of killing the pig and convincing him to let her keep and take care of it, which flips the mood to a positive mood.

The second chapter starts off with a positive mood, Fern's love for her rescued pig, Wilbur. But ends with a negative mood when Mr. Arable announces that the pig is big enough to be sold and Fern needs to sell it.

Chapter 3 starts off positive and then turns to negative but ends on a positive note. It begins by describing Wilbur's new home, a barn, as a pleasant place to be and tells how Fern visits Wilbur almost every day. But the mood changes when one day Fern doesn't come and Wilbur feels "lonely and bored." So Wilbur escapes, gets chased, and finally gets caught when he is lured into coming back by being offered some delicious-smelling slop. Once Wilbur eats it, he is glad to be home and forgets all about his loneliness and boredom.

The fourth chapter, entitled "Loneliness" (once again, mood drives the story!), starts with Wilbur in a horribly negative mood.

Table 5.6 is some of the textual evidence from the chapter that shows that Wilbur is in a negative space.

The negativity lasts nearly the entire chapter, until, at the very end, readers are introduced to the story's heroine, Charlotte, who gives Wilbur some hope.

> You can imagine Wilbur's surprise when, out of the darkness, came a small voice he had never heard before. It sounded rather thin, but pleasant. "Do you want a friend, Wilbur?" it said. "I'll be a friend to you. I've watched you all day and I like you."
>
> "But I can't see you," said Wilbur, jumping to his feet. "Where are you? And who are you?"
>
> "I'm right up here," said the voice. "Go to sleep. You'll see me in the morning." (White 1952, 31)

And that's the end of the chapter. Not only does this mystery voice make the reader want to turn the page to find out who it is, it also gives Wilbur hope for a better, brighter tomorrow. This chapter, like Chapter 1 of the book, has the same Mood Structure as *The Dot* (Reynolds 2003), and therefore strong-link connections can be made to that book, as well as to *The Lemonade War* (Davies 2007) and *The Tiger Rising* (DiCamillo 2001).

Another example of an author flipping a mood at the end of the chapter can be found in the Newbery Medal–winning *Bridge to Terabithia* by Katherine Paterson (1977). In the chapter entitled "The Perfect Day," after a bit of a dreary start (rain: color lens) and some yelling (sounds lens), Paterson spends most of the chapter crafting a jubilant mood for

TABLE 5.6

Text	Relevant Access Lens	Inference/Mood/Meaning
The next day was rainy and dark.	Color	It's a gloomy sort of day.
Templeton was nowhere to be seen.	Far apart	Wilbur is feeling lonely.
"Are you out there, Templeton?" called Wilbur. There was no answer.	Silence	This heightens the sense of loneliness.
. . . Fern won't come in such bad weather.	Far apart	Wilbur wants a visitor.
And Wilbur was crying again . . .	Action	Wilbur feels sad that nobody was around.
Wilbur did not budge.	Inaction	Depressed
Darkness settled over everything.	Color, symbol, big	There was no hope anywhere.

the main character, Jess. He and his favorite teacher spend the day at a couple of museums, just the two of them (close together lens). What started as a rainy, miserable day turns into a gorgeous day. Paterson writes, "When they came out of the building, it was into brilliant spring sunshine" (100–101). Shortly after, they step into the sunshine (color lens), Jess thinks to himself, "This one perfect day of his life was worth anything he had to pay" (big lens; 101). And pay he does, for at the end of the chapter his sister tells him, "Your girl friend's dead . . ." (102).

You might have noticed that the mood in this last example changes from negative to positive and back to negative. Even though this isn't one of the three Mood Structures that I introduced in Chapter 4, students can still use their understanding of the other Mood Structures to identify and interpret the sequence of mood changes in this chapter. This is a good example of how the components of AoC are not meant to be absolutes: they are tools to help students to notice, to think about, and to discuss the information that artists and authors provide and how this information is presented. Regardless of Mood Structure, understanding that moods change in stories and having a general sense of how this happens goes a long way toward helping students to meaningfully think about all the texts they encounter.

USING TEXTS FROM PICTURE BOOKS

In Chapters 2, 3, and 4, I focused on how to use artworks and illustrations along with the tools of AoC to engage students in making meaning. In this chapter, I've focused on helping students to use AoC to make meaning of written texts. What I have not mentioned is the value of using picture books to help students transfer their thinking around visual texts to written texts. Since picture books have both pictures and words that often share similar information, students can use them to learn how the skills of looking at pictures can be applied to written texts.

A favorite book that demonstrates how to apply picture book skills to written text is *The Other Side* (Woodson and Lewis 2001). In general, the pictures in this book meet my requirement of conveying similar information as the written text, which makes it easy for students to use the Access Lenses to think about the Framework with both the words and the pictures. When I use this book, I like my students to explore the pictures first through a mood walk (as I outlined in Chapter 4). Next, we go through the book page by page, comparing the illustrations with the written text, discussing how the mood is shown through each.

PLOTS AND SUBPLOTS

Subplots create space for authors of novels, plays, operas, movies, and television shows to craft a story's roller coaster of mood. Most picture books, such as *The Dot* (Reynolds 2003) and *Ish* (Reynolds 2004), don't have subplots. Even when they have multiple characters that impact the main character, these relationships don't evolve into separate storylines, which means we can represent the structures of these books using a single Mood Structure.

With stories that do have subplots, numerous storylines are developed, like mini-stories within the main story. For example, the passages I quoted from *The Lemonade War* and *The Tiger Rising*, which each show the Mood Structure of negative to positive, deal only with the main plot. The subplots have their own Mood Structures and enable the author to show characters that have various moods throughout the story. Thus, they help readers get a fuller sense of the characters, as well as allowing them to experience the plot from different angles, which can make a story more sophisticated and more interesting; however, for some students, subplots can make the story harder to follow.

In this case, the Mood Structures can be used to analyze, to think about, and to discuss the plot and each subplot separately. Mood Structures help students better organize the story, which makes it easier for them to think about where the story is and where it might be going. This may sound like sophisticated work for young readers to do, and it is, but when students start to engage with sophisticated texts, they will have to manage several storylines to comprehend the text fully. Using the components of AoC can help them begin to do this work.

A great example of various storylines having different Mood Structures within a single story is the animated movie *Frozen* (Buck, Lee, and Morris 2013). The main plot is the story of two royal sisters, Elsa and Anna. At the beginning of the movie, they start off playing joyfully. But shortly into the story, their relationship becomes strained and then sours altogether. By the end, however, an act of true love brings the sisters close again. The main plot of *Frozen* can be represented using the Mood Structure positive to negative to positive.

But Anna is also involved in two major subplots that set up the twists and turns within the story. The first involves a fellow royal named Hans and helps to create the tension between Anna and Elsa. This subplot starts off wonderfully. Hans and Anna fall madly in love almost instantly; things couldn't be better between them. Any guess where this subplot is going? If you predicted downward, you were correct, and so this subplot can be represented by the Mood Structure positive to negative.

The second subplot involves Anna and Kristoff, a solitary ice salesman whose only friend is a reindeer. This subplot starts off with arguments and conflict. Things couldn't be worse between the two characters. Can you predict how it winds up? If you predicted things getting better, then once again, you are correct. This subplot can be represented by the Mood Structure negative to positive.

Using the Mood Structures to analyze each plot and subplot allows students to understand how the story was crafted and how each part of the story fits together. Once students have a handle on determining moods and the Mood Structures, understanding plots becomes more straightforward. Having a sense of how stories are constructed goes a long way to aiding comprehension. Many stories and texts that students engage have similarities that can become fertile ground for making numerous strong-link connections. Learning how moods are crafted and applying the Mood Structures are good means for students to make these kinds of connections, using their background knowledge to make meaning of the texts before them.

AoC AND NONFICTION OR INFORMATIONAL TEXTS

Imagine a cat that feels threatened. Did you picture its face with its teeth exposed? Did you picture its body with its back raised? Did you hear its hiss? Now, picture a big cat on the hunt in the African plains. What's the mood? Is it tense? Is the cat's color important? Can you picture the cat's body language? Can you picture its actions? Is the cat making any sounds? Are there sounds when it chases its prey? When it catches its prey? Are the cat's big paws or big teeth important? Does it start off close to its prey or far from its prey? Is it with other cats, or is it alone? Is its prey in a herd or solitary? Is the cat a symbol of power and agility? As these events unfold, did the mood change at all? Is what you pictured real or fictitious?

As you can see from this thought exercise, elements of AoC can be applied to factual situations as well as to fictional ones. Even though we divide books by genre, in reality readers often experience strong similarities across those genres. Informational pieces may have narrative elements, and fictional pieces may have informational elements. Fiction writers sometimes research as much as informational writers, while informational writers are sometimes the best storytellers around. Genres are like ingredients that writers can use. Authors add a pinch of this or a cup of that to craft something delicious for the reader.

The stronger the narrative element is in informational writing, the easier it is for students to use all three components of AoC. Think of the story of General George Washington crossing the Delaware River on the night of December 25, 1776. Usually, this event is presented to students as a story filled with mood. It's easy for students to use all the components of AoC to think about the information. But even when students are studying a text that has almost no mood, the Access Lenses can still be used to help students notice, think about, and discuss the information before them.

HELPING STUDENTS GET STARTED USING AoC WITH INFORMATIONAL TEXTS

I introduce students to using the Access Lenses with informational texts the same way I do with narrative texts: with a visual text. When I introduced this idea to a group of second graders who were reading below grade level, we looked at a photograph of a naked mole rat on the cover of an informational book and used the Access Lenses to direct our attention and decode the image. Table 5.7 shows the information that the students noticed and the Access Lenses they used to direct them to that information.

After we noticed this information, the students thought about what it might mean by making predictions. Even if their predictions were general or even wrong, making them helped the students get ready to listen with purpose to the information in the book. To do this work, I guided the students to make connections between what they noticed and their background knowledge about other animals.

"I'm thinking about the big lens right now," I said. "I'm thinking that big things on animals are usually important. Can anyone think about something that is big on an animal that is important to them?"

"My dog has big ears," Crystal said.

"And why are your dog's big ears important to your dog?" I asked.

"Because dogs have really good hearing."

"Aah. That makes sense. I'm thinking of giraffes. What is big on a giraffe, and why is it important?" I asked.

"Their necks!" Peter and Rebecca shouted together.

"Turn and talk to your partner about why giraffes' long necks are important to them," I said.

After discussing why a giraffes' long necks help them reach food, we looked at the naked mole rat. "What do we notice that's big on the naked mole rat?" I asked. The students turned their attention to the naked mole rat's big teeth. Although they didn't predict that the teeth were important for digging, students speculated that their

TABLE 5.7

The Access Lenses	Information
Face, big and little	Big teeth, big nose, little eyes, little ears
Body	Skin, no fur
Color	Pinkish, whitish, brownish
Zoom out	Dirt around it

large teeth were important. This got them curious and ready to find out why from the written text.

Another connection that we focused on was the naked mole rat's lack of fur. With their partners, the students discussed other animals that don't have fur and why they don't need it. The students mentioned snakes and lizards and brought up the creatures' desert habitats. Their prediction was that maybe the naked mole rat lived someplace warm. As I read the written text, they listened eagerly to see if they were right.

We also talked about the naked mole rat's skin color. The students made a contrasting connection by noticing that, unlike snakes and leopards, the mole didn't have camouflage. Then they correctly predicted that naked mole rats don't need to blend in. This thinking and discussion prepared them for a rich conversation about why the naked mole rat didn't need camouflage once we found out that it lived underground.

By using the Access Lenses with this image, students were able to home in on relevant and revealing information, think about it, and engage in a productive discussion about it. Just as with fictional texts, when students can identify information that matches an Access Lens it's usually important information.

The components of AoC are tools for students to use. A hammer and saw, by themselves, won't build a house for a carpenter: the carpenter needs to know when to apply each tool. Similarly, the components of AoC won't build meaning for the reader. Readers have to learn to use the components of AoC in different ways when facing different situations. The previous example showed students mostly using the Access Lenses. Next, we'll look at how all three components of AoC can be used to explore an informational text.

The following passage is from an article entitled "Devastation in Vanuatu" (Blackburn 2015). As you read it, think about the mood the author is crafting and what Access Lenses you are noticing (or envisioning) that help you figure out the mood.

> Smashed boats, soggy piles of household items, and scraps of tin roofs litter Port Villa, the Capital city of Vanuatu. Over the weekend, major tropical cyclone Pam destroyed buildings and ripped down power lines in Vanuatu's capital city. The storm tore across the country's chain of more than 80 islands.

Even from the first sentence, students can get a sense of the mood: it's awful there. More specifically, the mood is one of chaos, violence, or devastation. Deconstructing these three sentences using the Access Lenses can help students notice, think about, and discuss the key information in the paragraph, which supports the idea that the mood is negative (see Table 5.8).

In this article, other than a few quotations from the president of Vanuatu, the people of Vanuatu aren't mentioned. However, students can get an even greater understanding of the article if they go beyond the text and use AoC to think about (or envision) the people who were affected by Cyclone Pam. Thinking about the moods of the people of Vanuatu is not only a great way for students to develop empathy, it also gives them another way to engage with the content of the article and to make meaning of it.

The first time that I discussed this aspect of the article was with a group of fifth-grade students. I used the Access Lenses to help frame my questions to get students to think beyond the text. One of the questions that I asked was, "How would the people feel when the cyclone was closing in on the island?" (close together lens). After students turned and talked, they shared their thinking. They came up with words such as *scared, nervous, worried,* and *uncertain*.

At times, I shared my thinking so that students could see how I was using the lenses to aid my thinking. I explained that reading the

TABLE 5.8

Text Evidence	Access Lens	Inference/Mood/Meaning
Smashed boats, soggy piles, scraps of tin roofs litter . . .	Big, symbols	It's a big mess. It represents destruction and devastation.
Smashed, destroyed, ripped, tore	Action, sounds, words	The sentences are filled with verbs that connote violent sounds and that are associated with destruction.
. . . chain of more than 80 islands.	Big	Eighty islands is a huge number of islands. The storm was large.
Cyclone	Symbols	Literally a symbol of destruction.

article made me think of the far apart lens. I then asked, "Right after the cyclone hit, what were the people far apart from?" Again, after the students turned and talked, they shared some of their thoughts.

"I think they are far away from comfort," Samantha shared.

"That's a great word! Why does Samantha's idea make sense?" I asked the group. "What evidence can we use from the text to support Samantha's idea? Turn and talk with your partner."

After about thirty seconds, I asked Xavier to share his thinking. "Well, Brian and I thought it made sense because the article said that buildings were destroyed and the power lines were ripped down and that roofs were all over the place. We thought this probably means that people's homes were damaged or even destroyed and that they don't have any power."

As you can see, asking questions like these, or having students use the Access Lenses to generate their own questions, helps students to bring their background knowledge to the texts they read.

Throughout the discussion, I used other lenses to formulate questions, too. For a few examples, see Table 5.9.

This article also has a clear Mood Structure. After describing some more of the destruction that the Category 5 cyclone (big lens) caused, the author changes course and brings in some symbols of hope and support. To show you what I mean, let's look at another passage. This one can be found closer to the end of the article, beneath a bold print heading, "A Helping Hand."

> Aid is also pouring in from countries near and far. Military planes from Australia and New Zealand have conducted fly-overs to help assess damage. Both countries, along with France, have also sent workers to help with disaster relief, including much-needed supplies.

After this section is decoded, students can use the Access Lenses to notice the information, grow ideas around the text, and make meaning of it (see Table 5.10).

When students have been working with AoC for awhile and they recognize that they can use an access lens to think about information in a text, a little bell should go off in their heads that this information is important. Once they had thought about the article through different lenses and noticed some areas where the lenses apply, the fifth graders could start to synthesize the information into coherent

TABLE 5.9

Question	**Access Lens**	**Potential Student Response**
What might the people look like as the storm hit? What would their faces and bodies look like?	Facial expression, body language action, or inaction	The people might be huddled together. Their eyes might be tightly closed. Arms might be around others or might be wrapping their own heads.
What colors do you envision as the storm approached? As it hit? After is left?	Color, close together	As the storm approached, the sky probably grew darker and darker.
What do you think it sounded like as the storm hit?	Sound	The wind was probably loud and constant. People could hear roofs being torn off and buildings crashing down. Trees and tree limbs could be heard cracking. Debris probably was crashing into things.

TABLE 5.10

Mood: Hopeful or perhaps relieved (relief)

Text Evidence	**Access Lens**	**Potential Inference/Meaning**
Aid is also pouring in . . .	Symbols, action, close together	Aid is a symbol of support. *Pouring* in means lots of aid is arriving and actually getting to the island.
Military planes . . . have conducted flyovers . . .	Symbols, action, close together	Military is a symbol of power and safety. *Flying over* means that they are actively trying to help and that they are by the islands.
. . . sent workers to help . . .	Symbols, action, close together	Workers are a symbol of support. They are at the island or they are on their way.

answers. Let's look at what students' answers might look like when the Framework is applied. Step 1, list everything you see (decode), has already been completed, so I'll start with Step 2.

Step 2. Determine the mood and support your thinking with text evidence

Potential student response: "The mood is hopeful or maybe even relieved. I think this because the article says that aid is pouring in and that there are workers coming to help. It also says that much needed supplies are arriving."

Step 3. Think about what is causing the mood

Potential student response: "People feel relieved and hopeful because the article says that aid is pouring in and that there are workers coming to help. It also says that much-needed supplies are arriving. This means that they may feel like they are not on their own alone. They are getting the help they need."

Step 4. Determine the big idea, topic, or theme

Potential student response: "I think the author wants us to be thinking about help and hope. Help has arrived and that is giving the people of the island some hope."

Step 5. Think about symbols and metaphors

Potential student response: "The workers and military are symbols of support because they are there to help the people on the island. The aid and supplies are symbols of hope because people may feel like the things that they need to survive are coming."

Step 6. Make a text-to-text, text-to-world, or text-to-self connection

Potential student response: "This reminds me of Hurricane Sandy when afterward the army came in to help clean up. Neighbors and friends also helped everyone out to make sure people had what they needed and places to stay if they couldn't be at their houses. As awful as Sandy was, it brought people together."

In visual texts and in written text, whether fictional or informational, the ways authors and artists show information, and the information that they choose to show, are often similar. A fiction author describing a character's angry face is not much different from a photographer taking a picture of a cat's angry face for an informational book or an actor depicting anger or an angry protester's face captured by a photojournalist or documentary maker. Although the reasons for the anger may be different, how it is shown will be highly comparable and students can use the tools of AoC to recognize and discuss these comparisons. *What's the mood? How do we know it? What's causing the mood?* As simple as these questions are, they can provide students a way to begin to look at nearly any text, regardless of its form or genre. And these tools not only can help students begin but also can be carried throughout a text and into students' own lives—helping them to continuously construct meaning of the information they encounter.

I always joke that I only teach two lessons: I teach students to pull information *out* of texts or to put information *into* texts. In the last few chapters, I have shown how students can use AoC to think about and discuss the texts they read. In Chapter 6, I'll show how students can use AoC to think about and craft the texts they create.

CHAPTER 6

Writing Through AoC

Writing is easy. All you do is sit staring at a blank sheet of paper until drops of blood form on your forehead.

Gene Fowler
American journalist

Even for professionals, writing can be a tumultuous experience. Writing can be hard. Teaching it is no easy task. It's a tall order for sure.

In a single chapter, it would be impossible to address all aspects of good writing. And the reality is, as English language arts teachers, you probably already know many of them. So the question of this chapter becomes, How can you help your students to engage their writing process and their writing more confidently, efficiently, and purposefully? The Art of Comprehension (AoC) offers several answers to this question. Just as AoC provides a clear path for students to enter into the texts they read, AoC also provides a clear path to help students to think about the texts they craft. This chapter will explain how.

Because the AoC tools are the same for reading and writing, the conversations around writing are similar to the conversations around reading. With AoC, as we move between the two, I don't have to ask students to make a giant leap; I only have to ask them to take a tiny step. Often, the step is so small that it's imperceptible, and it doesn't even seem like we are on a different path.

The mini-Framework offers a good example of one of these small steps. In reading, I want students to answer these three questions:

1. What's the mood?
2. How do you know what the mood is (pull out key details)?
3. What's causing the mood?

With writing, I revise the mini-Framework just a smidge. I want students to answer these three questions:

1. What's the mood?
2. What's causing the mood?
3. How can you show what the mood is (put in key details)?

That's a tiny step, right? When students use the tools of AoC with visual and written texts, without even knowing it, they've been engaging with texts like writers, studying craft and structure. Once they realize this, it's easier for them to switch to thinking about how to craft mood, key details, and Mood Structures in their own writing. All of our rich conversations around reading become resources for students to draw from.

Let's look at an example of a fourth-grade student, Jo, who used mood, Mood Structures, and the Access Lenses while writing to create a text that, although imperfect, is quite engaging. As you read it, use the Framework and the Access Lenses to analyze it, as we did with the professionally crafted texts in the previous chapter. The thinking we use to pull meaningful information out of the professional texts and break it apart is the same thinking Jo used to build up her piece.

MAGGIE

As I walked up to Maggie's door I felt a swish of cold fear sweep over me. It wasn't completely that I was afraid of my sister, it was more because I didn't know if what I was doing was right. As I turned the knob my hand started to cramp up and I could feel myself get sweaty all over. I didn't know what to expect. After all, I hadn't seen her in a while and didn't want her to get all angry that I would just barge in on her, but I had to see what she was doing in there.

And that's exactly what I did. I flew open the door. Silence. The only thing I saw was Maggie sitting slumpily near her window with stuffed animals surrounding her. Maggie wore a dark scowl. A very unhappy scowl.

She finally broke the silence. But instead of yelling or screaming, she just started crying. Ginormous tears rolled down her pale cheeks. I walked over and sat next to her.

For the first time in the whole move I actually knew what she was feeling. That feeling like there's nobody else in the world. That feeling like you need a friend.

"I need you to help me with something," Maggie blurted out. Her eyes were swollen from rubbing them.

"Excuse me?" I inquired.

"I need you to help me with something," Maggie repeated.

"What?" I questioned.

"We need to get the family back together," Maggie replied.

"And exactly how do you expect me to do that?" I asked.

"That's the part that you're going to figure out. Listen, Stephanie, you have to help me." Maggie begged. "So what do you say? Will you do it? Please!?"

"I guess," I shrugged.

"Do you promise?"

"I guess. I guess," My voice trailed off.

"You're the best!" she said as she gave me a big hug. Even though she was delighted and pleased, the sadness shown through her voice.

"I guess. I guess," I whispered again under my breath not sure if it was because I was flabbergasted from the hug or because I had no idea how I was supposed to save this family.

Jo did lots of great work in this writing. Her lead is good. It establishes the moods as nervous and uncertain in the beginning, and gives the reader an idea about what is causing the mood. She used the Access Lenses, such as silence, facial expressions, and action to show the moods. She built up the mood to create tension and changed the mood to relieve the tension. She then used the end of this scene to set up a new mood and establish another problem for her character. These are all devices we can find in many professionally written texts.

I don't expect every fourth grader to be able to write like this. Jo is a voracious reader and takes her writing very seriously. However, when I enter into any classroom and teach using the tools of AoC, I do expect that I can get students to engage with most of the writing components that Jo thought about. Since writing usually starts with an idea, let's begin there.

GENERATING IDEAS THROUGH MOOD

One of the hardest things to do for any creator is to figure out what they are going to make. As an art educator and as a writing teacher, I often see students stumble because of this first decision. It can be extremely difficult for students to do the kind of work that's expected of them if what they choose to make (or have to make) isn't something that they can really dive into and explore. Too often, students start off with a vague idea that proves to be a bad fit and is ultimately unworkable.

When a student starts off with a bad-fit idea, it's nearly impossible for them not to end up with an awkward piece of writing. It will be murky and muddy, rambling and runny. Loose not tight. Everyone, including the student, will know it's a mess. This doesn't build young writers' confidence, and it's certainly not going make them fall in love with writing. When students find themselves in situations like these, it's easy for them to see themselves as bad writers.

Although all writers ultimately have to develop an approach to writing that works well for them, AoC provides some general ideas that can be helpful to get workable ideas flowing. As you might have already guessed, the process starts with mood. Since stories are told through mood, helping students generate ideas for writing that have strong moods immediately gives them a purpose and something to write toward: building and showing the mood.

Creating anchor charts with your students can help them to think about people, times, and places in their lives that have strong moods, whether positive *or* negative. Some examples are shown in Figures 6.1–6.3.

Although students can generate ideas by thinking of people, times, and places separately, for many students, just like in professionally written stories, all three of these aspects can be developed in their stories. If a student writes about her dad as a special person, she might develop her writing around a *time* they went fishing, and *place* may play an important role in giving readers a clear sense of this event. The student may want to describe the peacefulness of their fishing spot and the excitement when they caught their first fish. Or the student may emphasize the specialness of the moment by explaining that she wouldn't trade that day with her dad for anything, even though she got up early and the house was cold and she was tired and miserable sitting on an uncomfortable pier.

FIGURE 6.1
Story ideas about people

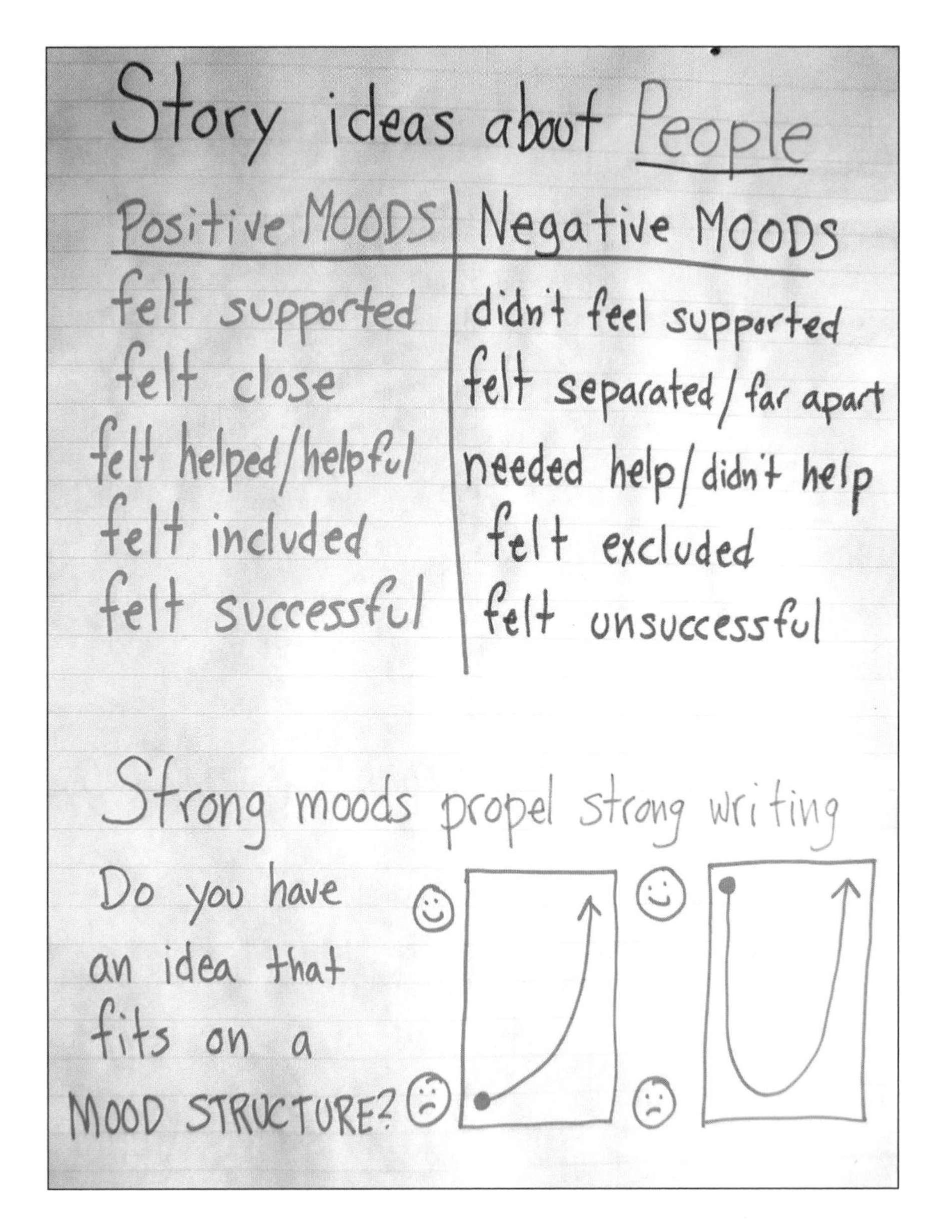

Guiding students to figure out the mood of their ideas gives them a thread with which to weave together the different aspects of their writing. A clear mood helps them in so many parts of writing—with leads, word choice, and elaboration. Every time they need to make a choice about any of these things, students can simply ask themselves, "What's the mood, and how can I show it?" The answers they come up

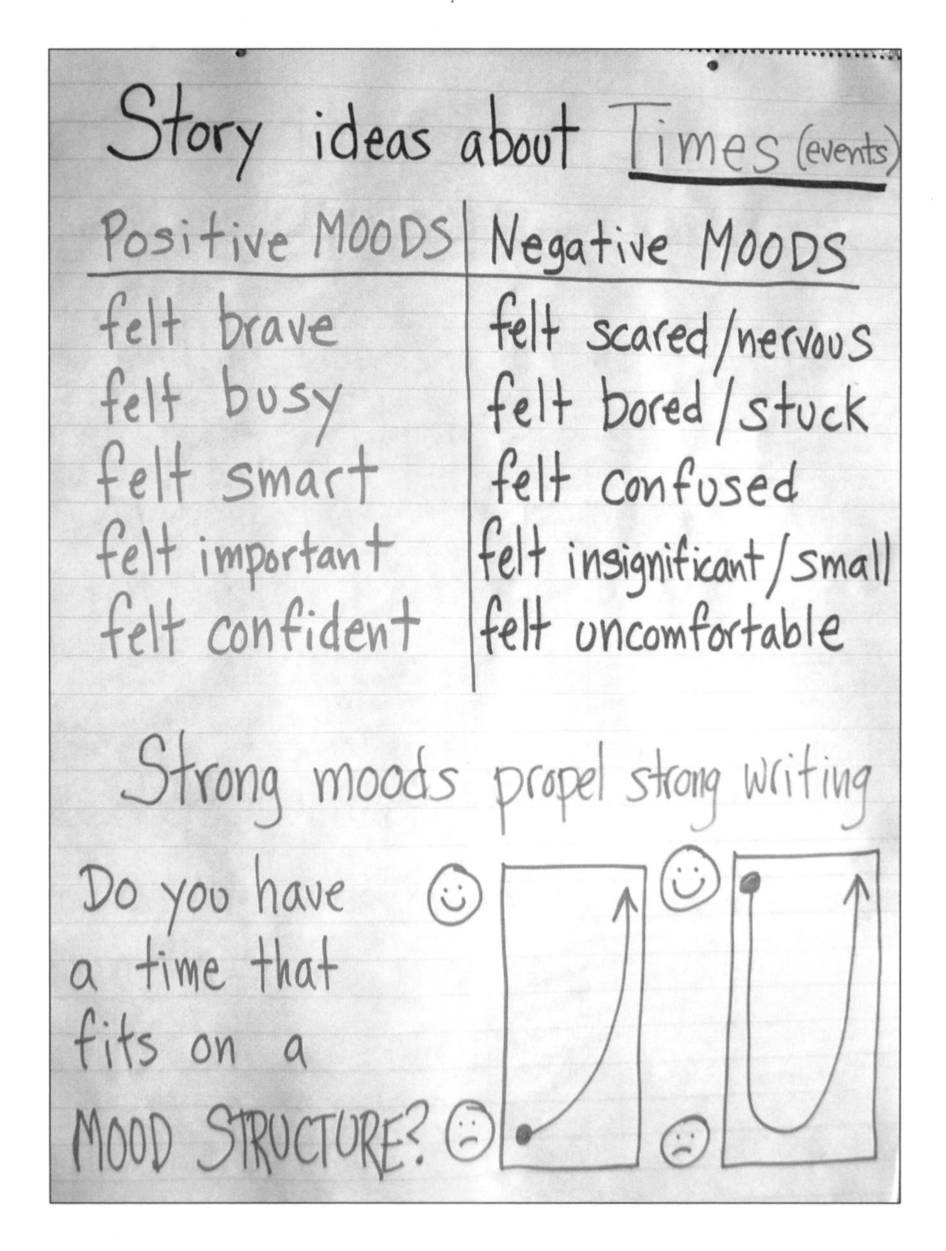

FIGURE 6.2
Story ideas about times

with will lead them toward making useful choices. Mood gives them a purpose. It gives them a destination to head toward. If students have a mood, then they have a map. How to move forward becomes a lot clearer. When students know the direction they are heading, it makes it a lot easier for them to step on the gas and go.

FIGURE 6.3
Story ideas about settings

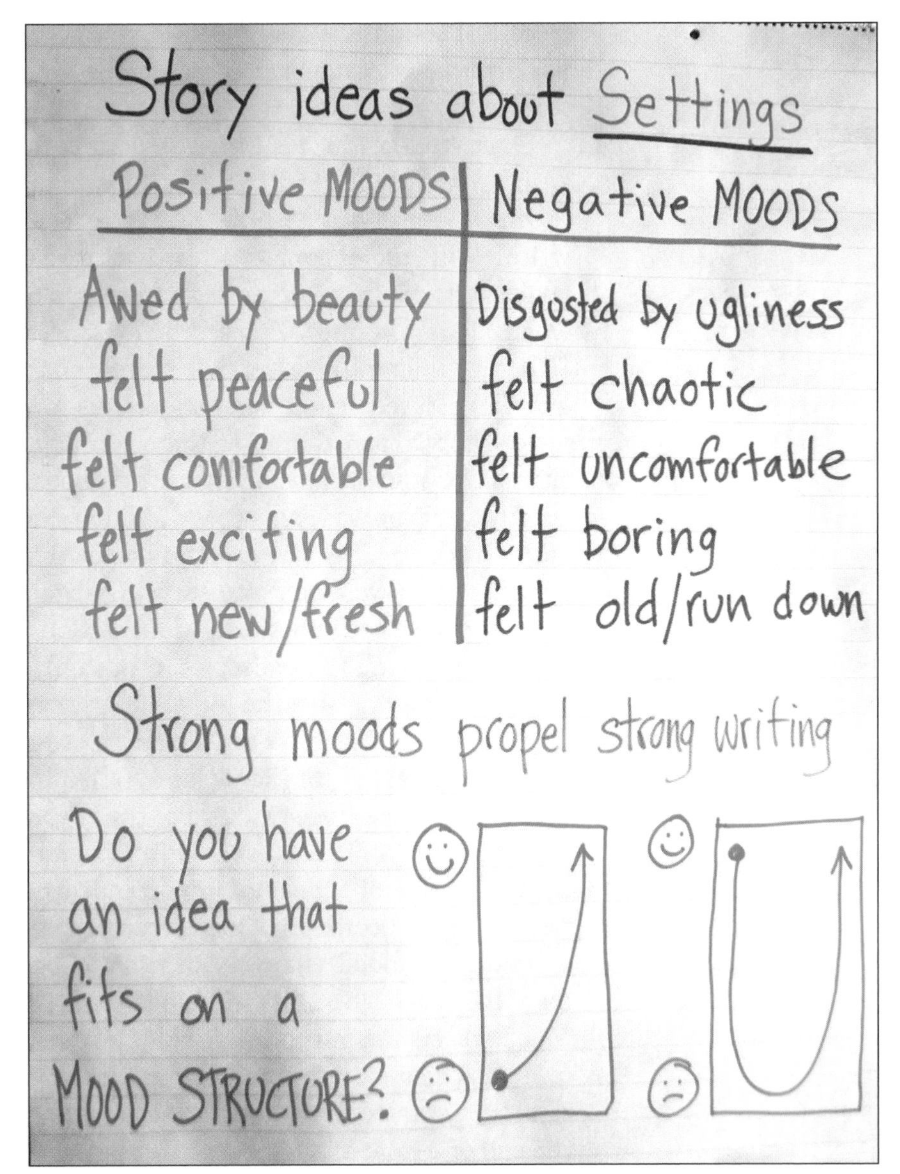

USING MOOD STRUCTURES TO SELECT IDEAS AND PLAN

When I confer with students about which of their ideas they may want to explore further, I focus on two areas. One, as we have discussed, is thinking about strong moods. The other is the Mood Structure. If students can align their story to a Mood Structure, then they know their piece will sound like a story. Since stories are told through mood and usually have at least one change in mood, when students structure their story with a Mood Structure, they are setting themselves up for success.

Once students have a Mood Structure, they can easily use any text with a similar Mood Structure as a mentor text. This allows the student to make lots of strong-link, text-to-text connections between their writing and professional writers' writing. Over time, this approach enables the student to pull ideas from lots of resources. Furthermore, when I look a young writer in the eye and tell them that their Mood Structure is just like a certain professional writer's Mood Structure and they can see that, it's an incredibly empowering moment for them.

Jo's story that I shared at the beginning of this chapter is a good example of student writing that uses Mood Structures. Jo didn't know exactly what she was going to write when she started, but she knew the basic structure. This gave her confidence that it could work. She knew her characters were going to start off distant and far apart and then become closer, both physically and emotionally. Jo also knew that this little scene wasn't the main plot; it was only a subplot, which gave her an opportunity to turn the mood negative again.

Although Jo's piece doesn't have the Mood Structures of *The Dot* (Reynolds 2003) or *Ish* (Reynolds 2004), it has a clear structure to it. It actually has the same structure as the chapter from *Bridge to Terabithia* (Paterson 1977) that I shared in Chapter 5—negative to positive to negative. Remember, it's not important that students always write stories that have a common Mood Structure; it's important that students are aware of mood changes both in the books they read and in the texts they craft. Jo's shift in moods shows that she understands this. Mood creates the tension that holds a reader's attention, and changes in mood often either resolve the tension so that readers can exhale or sometimes create new tension to drive the story further, as Jo did at the end of her piece.

If students have a Mood Structure in mind for their stories, or know that they will have different mood changes, then the Mood Structures can also be used to help students create an outline. Drafting an outline that lines up on a Mood Structure (or Mood Structures for more complex stories) can help students to see what each part of their story needs to do. Figure 6.4 shows an example of a student outline based on the same Mood Structure as *Ish* (Reynolds 2004).

Not every piece of writing is going to have a Mood Structure. Some written pieces are built around a single mood. For instance, if writing

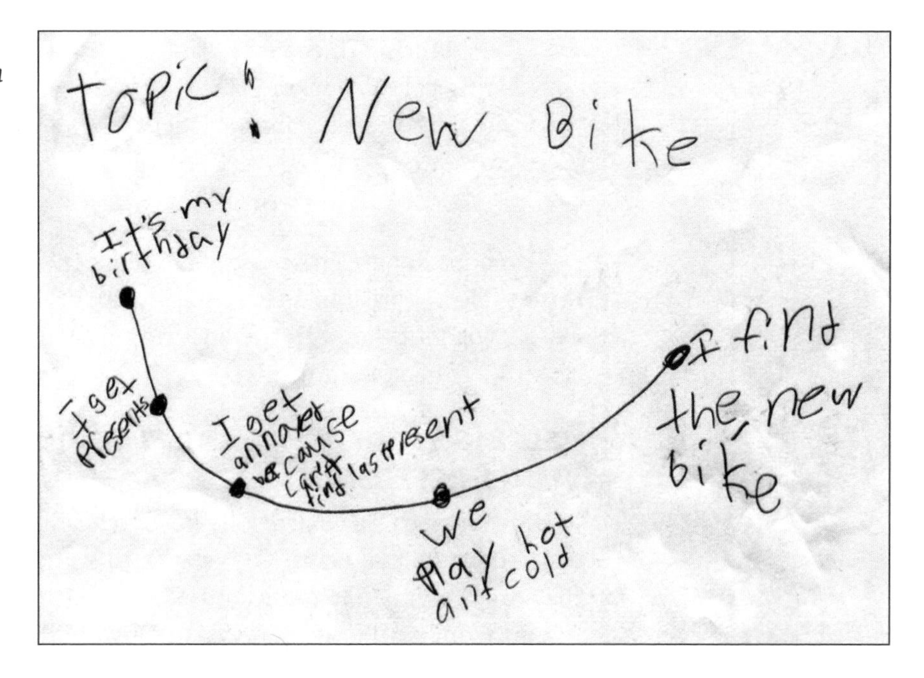

FIGURE 6.4
The Mood Structures can help students map out their story ideas.

about "The Best Day Ever!" the student might express excitement and joy throughout the whole piece. In addition, it is common for poems and articles to be crafted around a single mood. So an absence of mood changes is not necessarily a problem. One clear and well-conveyed mood may be enough if it suits the topic and genre.

WRITING WITHOUT MOOD

Some might argue that clear and well-structured writing doesn't always need a strong sense of mood. This is true. However, without creating a mood, the writing will rarely be captivating. To demonstrate this, let's look at another piece that Jo wrote. Although she tells the mood, in this piece, she doesn't use the Access Lenses to show the mood. Her writing is clear, but it is also quite dry and reads like a list without much spirit.

DANCE

I love to dance. It is one of my favorite hobbies. I take classes every Tuesday and Friday. On Tuesday, I dance ballet for two hours and on Friday, modern, tap and jazz for three hours. When [I] dance I feel wonderful! It's what I love to do. I have

> been dancing since I was 4 and never stopped. I go to dance at Spring Lake School of Dance. The teachers are so nice the lady who runs the place teaches there too. She was a former rocket [Rockette]!

The poet Robert Frost said, "No tears in the writer, no tears in the reader. No surprise in the writer, no surprise in the reader." In other words, without mood in the writing, the only mood in the reader will most likely be boredom.

HELPING STUDENTS TO CRAFT MOODS: VISUAL REFERENCES

To draw something well, artists have to be able to see it. There are three ways that artists do this. One way is to stand directly in front of what they are drawing. Plein air landscape painters do this. They stand outside in front of the scene and paint using direct observation. Another way that artists see is by picturing their subject in their head. Comic book artists and cartoonists often do this type of work. They see using their imagination. The third way that artists see is to use references, such as drawings or photographs that they can refer to. The reason I bring this up is because these practices can be applied to writing as well.

For writers to describe a setting, a character, or an object, they need to be able to see it. Unfortunately, many young writers only practice using their imagination while sitting in their classroom. Rarely, if ever, do students have the opportunity to write from direct observation or from references. If students have trouble envisioning what they are writing about, then they are at a great disadvantage. For these students, looking at illustrations, photographs, or even films can be a way to help them to see what they are trying to describe with words. And, of course, visual texts that reflect the moods that students are trying to craft can be the most beneficial.

HELPING STUDENTS TO CRAFT MOODS: DETAILS THAT SHOW

Once students have an initial idea, with a mood and perhaps with a Mood Structure, their next step is to think about crafting the mood (or moods). They need to ask themselves, "How can I show the mood?" Students already started thinking about how moods are crafted when they used the Access Lenses to pull key details out of any of the professionally crafted visual texts with which I introduced them to AoC. Afterward, they did the same thing with written texts to support their thinking around mood. Illustrators and writers, in words or pictures, articulate how faces, bodies, actions, colors, and so on show mood clearly, and students can learn these techniques from them. As my earlier chapters demonstrate, a lot of this work can be done with picture books you share with your students and with the texts you read to them or any of the illustrations or written passages that I've explored. If a student is writing about joy in their piece, they could use a graphic organizer (see Figure 6.5, page 96) filled in from the picture of Ramon in *Ish* (Reynolds 2004) or actually look at the picture, to help them think about how to *show* joy.

Notice how many different ways Reynolds shows Ramon's joy. I want students to understand that writers don't usually offer up one piece of information to help their readers understand and envision what is happening in a scene. They elaborate by providing numerous pieces that create a pattern for whichever mood they are portraying.

HELPING STUDENTS TO CRAFT MOODS: WRITING MOOD POEMS

The next part of the process is to help students use their knowledge of how moods can be shown to craft their own pieces. One activity that builds this bridge between reading and writing is what I call mood poems. I really like this activity because it clearly highlights the link between reading and writing or, as I sometimes say, comprehension and craft.

The first time I tried mood poems was with a fifth-grade class for which I had shown and discussed illustrations only twice for forty minutes each. In groups, they first determined a word or two that captured Ramon's mood on the first page of *Ish*. At this stage, they were practicing finding textual evidence to support their thinking about Ramon's mood and why he was feeling that way. Next, I asked them to use the Access Lenses to help them write sentences that show how Ramon felt. As they used the Access Lenses to notice the text evidence and wrote sentences based on it, they took a small step away from comprehension and into craft.

About halfway through their writing, the groups shared their poems so each group could hear how other groups were thinking about and presenting the information they were pulling out of the picture (see page 97). Through sharing, we expanded possibility for everyone, by giving them new ways to think about how to show the mood of joy.

Name: ______________________________

Mood/Change in Mood: Joyful

We can use the Access Lenses to help us think about and discuss the moods and text evidence in stories.

Colors	Bodies/ Action	Faces
Bright Cheerful Sunny Warm	laying on belly legs kicking painting	Smiling
Close Together Far Apart •close to artwork •far from being bothered •far from concern Alone alone	Words/ No Words Quiet No talking Peaceful Sounds/ No Sounds	Big Things stacks of drawings Concentration Little Things
Zoom in smile drawing squiggles Quiet, empty room Zoom Out	Symbol/Mood Drawing is happiness Drawing is joy	Connections Beginning of Purplicious Building with legos Reading

Determining moods, what's causing the mood and how and why these moods change helps us to think about and discuss stories more deeply.

FIGURE 6.5

Students can use a graphic organizer to help them think about showing any mood. If students or classes create these graphic organizers in writing, or use them during reading to analyze moods crafted in texts, they will have a whole library of moods, or mood reference sheets, from which to mine ideas.

RAMON (GROUP 1)

Ramon felt joyful
The room was so bright it lit up the night
A paintbrush was near
Ramon's face was full of focus
His eyes were wide open
His brush against the paper
Making lines here and there
With silence in the air
His legs kicking with excitement
They were moving everywhere
His painting was even brighter than the room
He felt like he had a friend in the world

RAMON (GROUP 2)

Ramon felt overjoyed
His eyes were wide open with curiosity.
His smile was as big as a banana.
His feet were kicking with a steady rhythm
Thump, thump, thump, thump.
The room was lit up with his joy.
He didn't need anything in the world except his paintings.

RAMON (GROUP 3)

Ramon felt peaceful
He had a big smile on his face.
He was close to his paintings like they were his best friends.
His legs were kicking with creativity.
His eyes bulging with joy.
Relaxing under the sunshine.

RAMON (GROUP 4)

Ramon felt love.
Not a care in the world for Ramon.
Ramon enjoys drawing.
Ramon likes using bright colors
Ramon's emotions are like candy.

In previous chapters, I discussed how the Access Lenses can help students to notice key details that help them comprehend the image and interpret its meaning. Through the mood poems, we see students begin to use the Access Lenses as cues to help them think about key information that they can include in their writing. In this way, the Access Lenses become a tool to help all students to clearly see the reading and writing connection, a connection that many of the best student writers have already made.

One of my favorite concepts in art making, whether creating a written text or some sort of visual text, is the idea that answers are found in the work. Once something is started and has taken form, then the creator and others can think about it, talk about it, get a sense if it is working, and decide what direction the work might go in. Once students create their mood poems, whether in groups, in pairs, or individually, we have things to talk about. Beyond discussing showing, not telling, the student's mood poems allow us to talk about many different writing elements, such as metaphors and similes, key details, word choice, patterns, leads, and elaboration.

HELPING STUDENTS TO CRAFT MOODS: WHOLE-CLASS WRITING

Another way to help all students explore crafting moods is by creating short passages as a class. In this exercise, I usually write the first sentence, which indicates what mood the passage needs to show. Then students work together to create additional sentences that show the mood using the Access Lenses. A few examples are shown in Figures 6.6 and 6.7. (In the first example, you'll notice that the word *tickled* is crossed out and replaced with the word *scratched*. This was the result of a quick lesson on how good word choice helps to capture the mood. You may also notice that the first example has a subtle change in mood, or a Mood Structure).

The branches ~~tickled~~ scratched my window. I pulled my blankets up to my chin. The wind howled. Lightning flashed. BOOM! Thunder roared. I heard footsteps in the hall. The branches scratched harder. The footsteps came closer and closer. I saw a shadow. The door opened slowly. Creeeeeeeeeeeeek.

Meow.

FIGURE 6.6
Students worked as a class and used the Access Lenses to elaborate and show the mood. Writing short stories like this can help all students with how to use the Access Lenses when crafting their writing.

FIGURE 6.7
Students worked as a class and used the Access Lenses to elaborate and show the mood in this paragraph.

HELPING STUDENTS TO CRAFT MOODS: WRITING LEADS THROUGH MOOD

As discussed in the previous chapter, a great way for students to enter into written texts is by determining the mood at the beginning, or lead, of a story, essay, or article. Young writers can also work to capture their readers' attention by establishing a strong mood in their leads. The Access Lenses can help them to do this. Since each lens can help to show moods, each lens can be a potential starting point for a strong lead sentence.

Let's quickly look at one of my favorite leads. It's from the book *The Cay*, by Theodore Taylor (1969). Students can use the Access Lenses to help them see and discuss how Taylor crafted the mood of danger (see Table 6.1). He starts his book with this sentence:

> Like silent, hungry sharks that swim in the darkness of the sea, the German submarines arrived in the middle of the night. (1)

TABLE 6.1

Text Evidence	Access Lens	Meaning/Mood/Inference
Like silent, hungry sharks . . .	Silence	Silent threats are scarier and more dangerous than louder threats because you can't tell that there is a threat or where it is coming from.
hungry sharks	Symbols	Hungry sharks are symbol of danger because hungry sharks are desperate and will attack in order to survive.
Darkness . . . middle of the night	Colors	Things we can't see (or hear) are dangerous. Nighttime can be a scary time.

By studying a lead like Taylor's in *The Cay*, students can see that one way to open a story is to establish a strong mood. By using the Access Lenses to notice key details within the lead that help establish the mood, students can see how they can use them with their own writing when trying to craft a lead of their own.

You can also use student writing to teach crafting leads through mood. Let's go back to the mood poems about Ramon. I shared the poems with a fourth-grade class about to begin drafting personal narratives. After reading them, they discussed with their writing partners which sentences could work well as an opening line. Their teacher, Mrs. Tice, and I asked them to pick a line that both captured their attention and that began to show a mood. Here are some of the sentences students were drawn to:

> His legs were kicking with creativity.
>
> His eyes were wide open with curiosity.
>
> The room was lit up with his joy.

After our discussion, we had the students work with partners to craft a three- or four-sentence paragraph that aimed to capture and show Ramon's mood by picking sentences from the mood poems or by creating their own. Essentially, they were writing a lead paragraph for *Ish* (Reynolds 2004) as if there wasn't an illustration. Here are a few examples from their first attempts:

> **1.** Ramon's smile as bright as the sun kicking his legs with no worry in the world. He feel's happy that he's alone because he is so into his drawing.
>
> **2.** Ramon's eyes were bulging with joy his painting was like his new best friend Ramon was so relaxed he was laying on the floor but he felt like he on the grass.
>
> **3.** Ramon had a smile from ear to ear. His face was full of focus. Ramon's room lit up with joy. His legs kicking with creativity. Ramon could not take a care in the world his painting meant everything to him. His eyes bulging with joy. Ramon was in deep concentration.

In all of these paragraphs, we can see some life, some spirit. There is a playfulness to them that tries to capture the mood and show it in interesting ways.

Next, students worked on an opening paragraph for their own stories. Mrs. Tice and I asked them to string a few sentences together that showed the opening mood of their personal narratives. The following is an example from a student who usually needs some support to start working:

> Steven was biting his nails wathing [watching] his teacher passing out tests to the students. When Mrs. Tise handed the test to Steven and a tear was falling out of his eye.

And here is an example from a student who tried to show a contrast between the weather and how his character feels:

> He walked through the fog to his bus stop with a smile on his face. He starts to see his friends through the thick mist.

The last example is from a student who didn't generate anything for the first half of the class. When Mrs. Tice had a chance to confer with him, she asked, "Okay, Cameron, so what's the mood you are thinking about?"

Cameron replied, "Relaxed."

"Great! You have a mood," said Mrs. Tice. "So what would your character's face look like, what could his body be doing? Could you use the picture of Ramon to help you think about how to show your character's mood?"

After briefly discussing these ideas, Mrs. Tice asked one final question. "What could your character say to himself to show how he's feeling?"

This is what Cameron wrote:

> Chris was watching TV on a Sunday kicking his feet and smiling calmly. "Best day ever!"

These pieces were written at the end of October, only the second month into the school year. Yet the pieces reveal students who are thinking like writers, adding key details that show moods and help readers to envision the scene being crafted. This is the power of helping students use the Access Lenses to pull moods out of the texts they are reading and to put moods into texts they are writing. Exploring leads offers a perfect opportunity to do this work.

CONFERRING THROUGH AoC

So far I have discussed how AoC can help students engage with idea generation, idea selection, outlining, elaboration, and leads. In this section, I'll explain how I use the tools of AoC to help confer with my students. As you will see, AoC enables my students to approach their writing the same way we approach the professionally crafted writing we read. This creates remarkable consistency that gives my students and me an easy way to talk more confidently and meaningfully about their work.

Whether chatting with students about their story ideas or their drafts, I keep the Framework in mind. Early in their writing, I generally focus on the mini-Framework, and, then, as the piece develops, we can use the full Framework to guide our conversation. Either way, the first question I ask is, *What's the mood?* and then, *What's causing the mood?* Students must know what their mood is and what's causing the mood if they are going to craft strong pieces. After that, I chat with them about how they can show the mood. We also discuss possible Mood Structures if their piece has any changes in mood.

The following is an example of a conference I had with a first-grade writer. In just a few sentences, many of the concepts previously discussed can be seen. This example was actually the first time I put my ideas about teaching writing through AoC into practice. It was thrilling to see how helpful AoC was. It allowed me to transact with the student's writing similarly to how I transact with professional writing, which provided clarity and consistency for the student and for me. Because the student was comfortable talking about mood and Mood Structures in the texts that we had read, she was also comfortable talking about these ideas in regards to her own work.

I pulled up a chair next to Kya, who was described by her classroom teacher as a writer who didn't have much confidence. When I looked at Kya's story, this is what I read:

> Elizabeth walked into the woods. It started to rain and thunder.

My first reaction was, "What am I going to do with this? There is hardly anything here." But I stuck to my plan and tried to focus on mood, the Access Lenses, and the Mood Structure.

I asked Kya, "So how did Elizabeth feel about walking into the woods?"

"Happy," Kya responded.

"Okay. So let's look at the Access Lenses and think about how you can show that Elizabeth is happy." We briefly discussed what her face could be doing, what sounds or words might show her happiness, and what actions might show a joyful mood. Although I didn't quite know what Kya was going to write, once I felt that Kya had an idea, we moved on to the next sentence.

"So did Elizabeth's mood change when it started to rain and thunder?"

Kya nodded yes.

Here was the mood change I was hoping for.

"And how did Elizabeth feel?"

"Scared," Kya said.

"Okay, so how could you show that Kya felt scared? What would that look like? How could her body change?"

Kya's eyes widened a bit, and she leaned toward her paper. Without even discussing it, she had an idea.

"You know what you're going to write?"

Kya nodded and continued to work. This is what she wrote:

> Elizabeth walked into the woods whistling. Elizabeth heard thunder. Elizabeth stopped whistling. Elizabeth froze.

Her story now was being crafted around moods. Not only that, but she never stated the moods directly, she simply showed them. Just before writing time ended, I shared Kya's beginning with her classmates. Based on the key details she had included, they correctly inferred that Elizabeth felt happy in the first sentence, and suggested "nervous" and "scared" for the last three sentences. As well as being a good, short reading lesson about inferring, it boosted Kya's confidence that her writing choices had worked.

Although I ran out of time, I could have conferred with Kya about using the setting to build up and show the mood. To get her to start thinking about this, I could have asked her, *Why does Elizabeth like going into the woods so much?* In response, it's not hard to imagine Kya describing the sunshine, singing birds, and flowers that Elizabeth saw and heard (the things causing the mood) as she whistled into the woods. Furthermore, it's also not hard to imagine her describing the darkness that overcame the woods as the storm rolled in. Because Kya had a clear sense of the mood that she was writing toward in her story, these conversations and additions would have been relatively easy.

Let's look at an example of a third-grade student named Sanjana who had been working on revision and elaboration.

When I peeked over Sanjana's shoulder into her writer's notebook, I saw an opportunity to help her push her writing. She had written her first sentence under the heading "Before."

> They said Jackson Jaguars won 1st place.

Her revised sentences were written under the heading "After."

> They said Jackson Jaguars won 1st place. We were so exciting and happy we got a huge trophie

When a student states the mood directly, they have a perfect opportunity to use the Access Lenses to help them elaborate and show the mood. So when I read, "We were so exciting and happy . . ." I saw an opening. I asked Sanjana, "What did you and your friends do then? What actions could show that excitement? What did it sound like? What did your faces look like?" She came up with three things:

1. Jumped up and down.
2. Screamed loud.
3. Giant smiles.

I also saw an opportunity to use the color lens to add details that would help her readers envision the scene. I asked her, "What did the trophy look like? Was it gray and dull?" I asked this last question to try to lead her. She took the bait.

She said, "Nooo. It was gold and bright and shiny!"

"Write that!" I said. "You got it. Your reader can see that. That will help them to envision your story."

I left her alone and moved on to confer with another student. When I came back, this is what Sanjana had written:

> They said Jackson Jaguars won 1st place. We were so exciting. We jumped up and down We scremed lound and had giant smiles on our face we got a huge trophie. It was gold, bright & shiny. It was amazing

Now Sanjana's piece had some life, some energy. Her readers could begin to feel what that moment was like and envision it. More important, Sanjana herself had felt her writing come alive. I shared Sanjana's three pieces of writing with her classmates. After I read her third revision, some of her classmates actually gasped in awe. At that moment, Sanjana's smile was probably bigger and brighter than the trophy her team had won.

By focusing on mood, Sanjana was able to revise and elaborate purposely. As a class, students were able to discuss what the mood was, what caused the mood, and what Access Lenses Sanjana used to show the mood the way we had previously analyzed professional writing. And by reading her work, we were able to help her classmates think about their own writing, taking tiny steps, moving between comprehension and craft.

A QUICK NOTE ON WORD CHOICE

Let's revisit the first grader Kya's writing again. Her first sentence would have presented a great opportunity to talk with her (and perhaps the class) about word choice. Kya wrote:

> Elizabeth walked into the woods whistling.

Kya wanted to show a happy mood. And although she was successful, she could have changed the word *walked* to something a tad more upbeat. Perhaps *twirled, danced,* or *skipped* would have shown the mood more clearly. Sharing this sentence with the class and having them think about words that could show Elizabeth's mood more clearly than *walked* creates a good opportunity for students to meaningfully engage the idea of word choice. Good word choice isn't about a ten-dollar word versus a five-dollar word: words don't have to be fancy. Good word choice accurately captures the mood that is being crafted.

QUESTIONS TO HELP STUDENTS THINK ABOUT THEIR WRITING

James A. Michener, Pulitzer Prize–winning author, is quoted as having said, "I have never thought of myself as a good writer. . . . But I'm one of the world's great rewriters." Revising is one of the most, if not the most, important parts of writing for students to learn. It also can be difficult to do and teach. Focusing on mood and using the Access Lenses can help. Once students have drafted an idea, when they revise, they can ask themselves these questions for each mood they introduce:

1. Do I have a clear mood?
2. Have I shown my mood through different lenses?
3. Can I use another additional lens to show it, too?
4. Do all of my words support the mood?

Students can also use these questions when they read their classmates' writing, and they can help you when you are conferring with your students. These four questions should be applied to each section of writing that aims to show a distinct mood. These questions are helpful for two reasons. First, they are concrete. They require a yes or a no answer. If a student can't answer one of these questions yes or no, then you have a good topic for a conference, mid-teaching point, or a minilesson. Second, these questions are broad. They can be applied to numerous kinds of writing, creating consistency across genres.

DRAWING THROUGH MOOD

For young students, striving students, or students who are including illustrations (or photos) in their writing, conferring through mood and the Access Lenses is still very much applicable. Just as we were able to deconstruct Peter H. Reynolds's artwork through the Framework and the Access Lenses, students can reflect on and craft their own drawings and artwork in the same way.

The drawing in Figure 6.8 was done by a five-year-old boy named Owen. When I conferred with him, I focused on mood and the Access Lenses. This made it easier for me to give him some targeted feedback on his work, pointing out a few things that he had done and helping him to try out a new idea.

He told me that it was a drawing of him and his friend John swimming in the ocean. Then I said, "You guys were having fun together, right?"

Owen nodded yes.

"You know how I could tell?"

Owen shook his head no.

"I could tell by your faces. What did you do with your faces that showed me you were having fun?"

"I made smiles," Owen said.

"Yep. I could tell by the big smiles. I could also tell because you drew you and John right next to each other. It also looks like a beautiful day to play. You know why I think that?"

"The sun," Owen said, putting his finger on it.

"Exactly. The bright sun helps me think about how happy you and John were."

"Were you just standing there or were you playing?"

"Splashing," Owen said.

"Maybe you could show some splashing in your picture? How could you do that?" Owen didn't know how to draw splashing so I gave him a suggestion.

Owen picked up his blue crayon and added some marks around him and John.

FIGURE 6.8
Owen's drawing of himself and his friend John playing in the ocean. We can use the Access Lenses to think about and discuss how moods can be crafted in students' drawings and illustrations.

To show the mood of his picture, Owen had instinctively used the facial expressions lens, the close together lens, the color lens, and, after a little discussion, he incorporated the action lens. These are the same lenses that we used to make meaning of the Peter H. Reynolds (2004) drawing of Ramon and the R. L. Stine (2013) passage regarding Bree's worry. At age five, Owen was thinking about and communicating mood using the same means as professional illustrators and writers. Not bad for a little guy.

I didn't have a copy of *Ish* (Reynolds 2004) near me, but if I had, it would have been easy for me to show Owen all the similarities between his work and the page of Ramon happily drawing. The image of Ramon would have helped Owen to think even more about these details when he draws and when he reads.

CRAFTING MOOD CHANGES TO HOOK A READER

As I explored in Chapter 5, the ends of chapters or scenes tend to bring about a change in mood. These changes are often key moments and can ratchet up the tension and drama. If students can learn to craft their own mood changes well, they have a powerful tool for captivating their audience, whether they are writing a story, filming a movie, or speaking to an audience.

Kya, the first grader, had a strong mood change in the beginning of her story about Elizabeth walking into the woods. Through it, her reader can feel the tension. The following passage is another example of a student who crafted a dramatic mood change. By the end of it, the reader definitely wants to read on and find out what happens. This narrative piece is by Harry, a fifth-grade student. As you read it, use the Framework and the Access Lenses to help you to think both about comprehending this piece and about how it was crafted. Think about the Mood Structures, too. Are there any strong-link connections you can make to some of the professional texts we've looked at?

THE BAD BEGINNING

I know it sounds wrong, but my family is as messed up as it could possibly get. Lets just say we're like clothes who took a trip through the washing machine and come out all tangled and twisted. But let me start from the beginning, let me tell you the whole story, the true story.

It was September 16, 1992. It was my birthday. It was a rainy Monday and summer was ending, but it was my birthday and nothing was going to ruin that.

Mrs. Noells voice rang out of the loud speaker, "Dean Zinger please report to the office."

I walked out the door thinking that they were just going to tell me happy birthday and send me out the door with a pencil or something. I thought about how my cheeks were going to get red.

> That always happens, but it was my birthday and I wasn't going to let that bother me.
>
> When I got to the office, what they told me was not happy birthday, and instead of giving me a pencil it was as if they stabbed me with one. My cheeks didn't turn red, they turned white. Suddenly, the fact that it was my birthday didn't matter, and I felt like one of the raindrops outside splattering on the sidewalk.

In this passage, Harry starts by establishing a negative mood regarding the character's family. But then Harry begins to tell the story and abruptly changes his character's mood to positive in part by having his character repeat that nothing, not the weather nor a little embarrassment, could ruin his day because it was his birthday. Then, wham! The mood changes yet again, and the reader is now brimming with curiosity to find out what caused the mood to change. What did they tell Dean Zinger that wound up ruining his day?

Besides changing moods to help hook his readers, Harry made some other choices regarding mood that helped him craft this engaging start. Let's look at a couple of these choices next.

USING MATCHING MOODS AND CONTRASTING MOODS

Becoming aware of how settings can either match a character's mood or form a contrast to it can help students with both comprehension and writing. In most of the texts we've looked at, the setting described matched the main character's mood and, therefore, helped to show it. The overcast, foggy weather matched Rob's gloomy mood in the beginning of *The Tiger Rising* (DiCamillo 2001), and the sunshine and blue skies matched his hopeful mood at the end. The dark basement and "the giving-up" kind of weather matched Evan's mood in the beginning of *The Lemonade War* (Davies 2007), and the fireworks matched the celebratory mood at the end of the book. The rain and darkness also matched Wilbur's lonely, forlorn mood in the chapter of *Charlotte's Web* (White 1952) we examined.

But in Harry's passage, we see a setting that contrasts with the mood. It's a dreary, rainy, September Monday, but Dean Zinger is happy nonetheless. Here Harry has deliberately and consciously used a contrasting setting to emphasize how strong the positive mood is: it implies that nothing could ruin Dean's day. This is skilled crafting. But the usefulness of the contrasting setting is even more prominent at the end, where it allows Harry to set up a more dramatic change of mood: if the bad news he receives can reverse such a positive mood as Harry has shown, then it must be really bad news indeed.

SIMILES AND MOOD

Good similes accomplish two things. They entertain the readers, which helps to hold their attention, and they can help to show the mood. Harry's simile at the end of his writing is a powerful example of this. "I felt like one of the raindrops outside splattering on the sidewalk" clearly shows the shattered mood with which Harry creates his change of mood and therefore creates a Mood Structure.

Good similes are created by making an interesting connection. Harry does this beautifully by connecting his character's mood to the splattering raindrops. (He also connected the end of this section of writing to its beginning.) Harry's work here is entertaining and effective.

CRAFTING MOOD ACROSS GENRES

In *Nonfiction Craft Lessons*, JoAnn Portalupi and Ralph Fletcher (2001) make the point that students should use what they know about fictional writing to enrich their nonfiction work:

> Human beings have been described as the "story species." And many students have a good sense of story. But when they move from narrative writing to informational writing, it seems that they leave behind everything they once knew about story. That's too bad because skilled informational writers draw on a wealth of fictional writing strategies (a sense of character, detail, suspense, and so on) to make their writing come alive. (88)

In the introduction to his memoir *Ugly*, Robert Hoge (2015) states the importance of story another way, saying, "Storytelling is the Krazy Glue that holds us all together. Stories can soar and sing and surprise. And sometimes . . . they do all three at once" (5).

Although these authors are writing about narrative writing in general, as opposed to moods, I hope that I have shown throughout this book that mood plays a huge role in crafting stories (narratives) that stick. So crafting moods is a way for students to enhance their writing in any genre. It may very well be that "storytelling is the Krazy Glue that holds us all together," but mood is the Krazy Glue that holds a story together.

Table 6.2 is a quick example of how a single mood (nervous) can enter into different genres of writing.

In each example, the writer would have to elaborate on the statement, declaration, claim, or opinion by providing supporting sentences. In this sense, structurally speaking, genres have a lot in common. Generally speaking, good writing is basically making some sort of statement (whether explicitly or implicitly) and then supporting that statement. If students first comprehend what good writing is in general and then afterward learn to apply their good writing skills to different genres, teaching different genres becomes a more efficient process. Helping students to see the commonalities between genres, as I have tried to do with written texts and visual texts, creates a strong foundation for this work with your writers (and readers).

TABLE 6.2

Genre	Sentence Example Integrating Mood
Narrative	I felt nervous.
Historical fiction	Martha Washington felt nervous.
Realistic fiction	Bill felt nervous.
Fantasy	My unicorn, Wally, felt nervous.
Science fiction	For the first time, Stevo 3000, the advanced android, felt nervous.
Informational/nonfiction	Scientists are nervous that . . .
Sports article (journalism)	The fans felt nervous.
Political article (journalism)	Her supporters were nervous.
Opinion	Roller coasters make me nervous.
Academic paper	The subjects appeared nervous.

WORKING MOOD INTO INFORMATIONAL/NONFICTION TEXTS

One way for students to hook their readers in informational writing is to start with a narrative based on their topic. And like all of the narrative writing I've discussed, these narratives can be crafted around mood by using the Access Lenses and Mood Structures, too.

In Chapter 5, using the Access Lenses, second-grade students pulled important information out of the picture of a naked mole rat (an informational text). The Access Lenses can also help all students think about what kinds of information to put into their informational piece. The following examples show how the Access Lenses can relate to information about owls:

Facial expressions

1. Big eyes
2. Sharp beaks

Body language/action

1. Can fly silently
2. Can turn heads almost 180 degrees
3. Talons

Colors

1. Come in different colors
2. Blend in with environment/camouflage
3. Like the cover of darkness/nocturnal

Close together/far apart/alone

1. Prefer woodsy areas
2. Solitary animals

Sounds/no sounds

1. Screech and hoot to communicate
2. Fly silently

Big/little things

1. Big eyes
2. Large woods/woods becoming smaller
3. Some owls are large/some small
4. Hunt small rodents
5. Big deal that they can fly silently

Zoom in/zoom out

1. Big eyes
2. Sharp talons
3. Special feathers for flying
4. Special ears
5. Blend in with the environment

Symbols

1. Owls are symbols of stealth

Symbols, destruction

1. Deforestation

Symbol, hope

1. Scientist and environmentalists working to save habitats

A lead that uses the components of AoC follows. When you read the passage think about the mini-Framework (both for reading and writing), notice which Access Lenses are used to show the various moods, and observe the Mood Structure of the short story.

OWLS

The owl sat patiently on the branch looking into the dark forest. She slowly turned her head to look behind her. Nothing. She waited. Finally, she heard a rustle. Her ears perked up. They moved ever so slightly until she knew exactly where the small

> sound was. Once the sound was located the owl spread her wings and silently flew through the forest. She gracefully twisted and turned, weaving through the trees, moving closer and closer to the tiny mouse scurrying beneath the leaves, searching for food of its own. In a blink of an eye, the mouse was airborne. It squeaked, as it was carried through the darkness, trapped in the owl's sharp talons.
>
> How can owls do this you ask? Well, owls are amazing animals. Let me explain.

This owl example is one that I wrote to share with the students and teachers that I work with. I created it to demonstrate how the Access Lenses can be used with nonfiction research and writing and how narrative, fiction writing can be woven into informational writing. In the following examples, two students did this work in their own informational pieces. The first is from a third grader who wrote about football. Here is his narrative opening:

> FOOTBALL
>
> I was in the hudle I was running back "power 6 on go power 6 on go ready break" I got in my potoin [position] I felt like I was in a desert of intencede [intensity] I was sweating nerves "ready set go!" I ran I got the ball I went through the 6 hole I spinned all around I saw the endzone but it was blocked off! But I tuck the[n] jumped over and . . . Touch down! Football is the most popular sport in america and this book is going to tell you all about it.

This next example is from a fifth-grade student who was introducing the topic about the Trail of Tears.

> TRAIL OF TEARS
>
> The gray skies were roaring. It was cold, they were bundled up.
>
> "We cannot last a whole week in these conditions." Someone said. Their faces looked down at their feet. Some of them tried to escape but it was nearly impossible. The ones who failed had to pay the price, death.

> Their faces were as gloomy as the sky. It started to rain and thunder. Babies were crying, people were tired and animals gave up. "None of us can keep on going," someone exclaimed. They all rested for the night. The sun went down and the stars lit up the night. "Will all of us make it out alive?" a kid asked. No one answered. The sun came up, people started moving and stuff had to be left behind.

As I discussed earlier, one strategy to help students to generate ideas that would make good stories or leads is to think about situations that have a strong sense of mood. Helping students to think about writing these leads was no different. To prompt students to consider how they might begin their narratives about their topic, I asked them to focus on the most emotional aspect of it. We then discussed what they thought. Scoring a touchdown in football and the harsh conditions along with the threat of death that the Native Americans had to endure certainly are loaded with emotion and provided ample material from which to craft interesting and dramatic leads.

USING THE ACCESS LENSES GRAPHIC ORGANIZER WITH NONFICTION

Figure 6.9 is an example of using the Access Lenses graphic organizer to explore a nonfiction topic. A fourth-grade class put together this example of an informational piece about soccer. It was chosen by a student who was having trouble getting started. Filling in this graphic organizer as a class accomplished two things. First, students helped their classmate come up with ideas. Second, students practiced using the graphic organizer to push their thinking around a topic, which was helpful when they thought about their own topics.

Once students fill out the Access Lens graphic organizer, each lens can potentially become a subtopic for their informational writing. Students might write about *action*, such as how animals or athletes playing a certain sport move. They might write about *colors*, such as why animals' colors are important or the various colors of uniforms. They might write about *sounds*, such as the sounds animals make or what sounds are associated with certain sports (silence in golf for instance). Using the graphic organizer in this way won't necessarily work easily for all topics, but for many students, it will provide a good start to help them to push their thinking and to organize their ideas and research.

FIGURE 6.9
The Access Lens graphic organizer can be used to think broadly about a nonfiction topic. We filled this example out as a class to help students learn to use it.

Once filled out, it also provides a word bank that can be helpful when writing and to possibly spark more ideas.

ACCESSING TONE THROUGH MOOD

As students become sophisticated readers and writers (creators), paying attention to tone can help them with comprehension and craft. To introduce tone to readers, think about it as author's mood. Let's look at the opening sentence to the book *The Worm* by Elise Gravel (2012). Gravel writes, "Ladies and gentlemen, I present to you THE WORM" (5). What's the author's mood? Playful? Silly? What does this sentence tell us about how the author feels about worms? Perhaps, that they are wonderful or amazing, worthy of a fancy introduction. Based on the author's tone, what can we expect to learn from this book?

Determining an author's mood toward a particular topic helps students to think about an author's purpose and presentation choices. Realizing the tone of authors and other artists can help students discuss how and why or whether a particular presentation approach is effective. Is the author excited, exasperated, worried, serious, playful, silly, or sarcastic? If students can determine the author's mood, it gives them an additional way to think about the content and what the author is trying to communicate.

Furthermore, once students understand that authors actually choose the mood (tone) of their piece, it opens up room for them to develop their individual voice. Ralph Fletcher models these two ideas in his book *Joy Write*, as he muses about writing about octopuses. Fletcher writes:

> Recently I read several articles about the octopus as escape artist . . . These articles sparked my imagination. I started thinking; perhaps I should try to write about these intelligent creatures. But how? . . . What form could it take? . . . A straight nonfiction feature article? Picture book? Chapter book? Playful essay? Collection of poems? Mock interview with the octopus itself? A story? Would it work best to tell it from my own perspective, or that of a naturalist, or perhaps from the octopus's point of view? How might it read? What would be my ultimate purpose? To entertain? Make people laugh? Inform? Persuade restaurants to stop including octopus and calamari on their menu? Or perhaps a combination of several ideas? (2017, 29)

Although Fletcher wasn't discussing tone directly, tone or mood is suggested through many of these questions. Considering genres and tones gives students a chance to think about presenting content in various ways, helping them explore, develop, strengthen, and differentiate their voice—important work for any developing writer or artist. The tools of AoC won't always necessarily help students determine the tone of the author, but being comfortable and familiar with the idea of mood will help even young students to grasp and discuss tone and how it can impact communication, including their own.

Final Thoughts

When I first started developing the Art of Comprehension (AoC), I saw it as a way to improve students' reading comprehension so that they could perform better on tests and meet reading-level requirements. I had a very limited understanding of why helping students to develop their comprehension skills was important. However, once I started digging into AoC and researching the teaching of comprehension strategies more purposefully, my thinking began to change. The following passage from Louise Rosenblatt is the passage that, without a doubt, influenced me the most.

> Certainly to the great majority of readers, the human experience that literature presents is primary. For them the formal elements of the work—style, structure, rhythmic flow—function only as a part of the total literary experience. The reader seeks to participate in another's vision—to reap knowledge of the world, to fathom the resources of the human spirit, to gain insights that will make his own life more comprehensible. (1995, 7)

Although Rosenblatt was writing about literature, her thinking can easily be applied to all of the arts. It's not the formal elements that drive most people's enjoyment of them; it's that the arts help us to comprehend and connect to our human experience. They help us to explore, to understand, and to celebrate our lives, our humanness. Although I had engaged with the arts my whole life, I was missing this clarity. Without it, all that I had to work with were the formal elements, the "right" answers, the test scores, and the reading levels. None of which were going to help my students to fall in love with the arts or, more important, to use the arts to make sense of their own lives and to help others make sense of theirs.

I've come to see life as a constant cycle of comprehension (making sense of the information we explore and take in) and creation (using that information to explore and communicate ideas). Within this cycle, the more students comprehend, the more they can create, and the more they create, the more they can comprehend. Helping children meaningfully engage with this cycle is, I believe, the most important work we can do as educators and parents. The arts provide an extremely efficient way to help students to meaningfully enter into this cycle. But to fully utilize the arts (reading and writing included), to take advantage of all they have to offer, we need a way to help all students to think about and discuss them deeply, meaningfully, and purposefully. *The Art of Comprehension* helps to do exactly this. AoC provides valuable tools that can help students to make meaning of the texts they engage with and then use this understanding to craft meaningful texts, texts that can potentially resonate and reverberate.

The Art of Comprehension has completely changed my life. Whether it's a book, a painting, a film, or some other form of artwork, AoC has giving me a way to share the joy that I find in the arts with my students and colleagues as well as a way to talk about how all of the arts can be used to improve students' academic lives. AoC has freed a world that once only existed within me. Likewise, it's helped free the ideas that seemed stuck inside many of my students and colleagues, too. I'm grateful that I've been able to share my voice with so many, and I'm also grateful for all the voices that have been shared with me. Thank you for taking this journey with me through the arts in general and the Art of Comprehension in particular. I hope you and your students will find it as powerful and freeing.

Appendix A: Reproducible Access Lenses

the ACCESS LENSES

Thinking about **MOODS** is an excellent way to access a text.

Artists, Writers & Performers show **MOODS** using the following information...

Don't forget to make strong connections through moods, lenses and symbols.

Name: ________________________________

Mood/Change in Mood: ________________________

We can use the Access Lenses to help us think about and discuss the moods and text evidence in stories.

Colors	Bodies/Action	Faces
Close Together Far Apart Alone	Words/No Words Sounds/No Sounds	Big Things Little Things
Zoom In Zoom out	Symbol/Mood	Connections

Determining moods, what's causing the mood, and how and why these moods change helps us to think about and discuss stories more deeply.

Name: ______________________________

Topic/Mood: ______________________________

We can use the Access Lenses to help us think about and discuss the topics we are exploring and working on.

Colors	Bodies/Action	Faces
Close Together Far Apart Alone	Words/No Words Sounds/No Sounds	Big Things Little Things
Zoom In Zoom out	Symbol/Mood	Connections

Remember that capturing and communicating the mood of your topic will help bring it to life.

Appendix B: Trip to the Museum

The following story is designed to help your students to engage the components of the Art of Comprehension (AoC). Both the illustrations and the text were crafted very deliberately with the components of AoC in mind, so when exploring it, students have lots of discoveries to make about mood, mood structures, and how moods are shown. Furthermore, the story itself walks the characters through using the Access Lenses with the Framework, thus providing an overview of what a conversation using AoC looks like when transacting with a visual text. Because of this, the book can be interactive. When the character, Ms. Brice, who is facilitating the discussion in the story, asks the student characters to engage the painting, your actual students can do the same work. They can essentially be on the tour along with the students in the book.

Beyond taking the museum tour, there are several other ways for you and your students to use this story and the accompanying illustrations. There is no singular correct way, and I would encourage you to visit it several times so that your students can explore it in different ways in order to grow their thinking and ideas around it. Your students can also explore it as a full class read-aloud, in small groups, with partners, or independently. Here are a few ideas:

1. Explore the first illustration using the Framework and the Access Lenses to practice noticing key details, using text evidence to support thinking and discussing texts using AoC.

2. Explore the beginning of the story and the first illustration to help students see the connection between visual texts and written texts.
3. Use the mood structures to map the story structure.
4. Compare and contrast the first illustration and the last illustration through mood and the Access Lenses (noticing how they flip).
5. Read the story and have students notice the Access Lenses that were used to craft the different moods within the story.
6. Use the graphic organizer to practice pulling out and recording key details that support the different moods in the text and illustrations.
7. Write mood poems using the illustrations (and/or text).
8. Have students make strong-link text-to-self connections and write about what they would like to escape from and what or who their yellow balloons are.
9. Students can also make strong-link text-to-text connections and write about the ideas of escape and yellow balloons in regards to their favorite characters from books or movies.

TRIP TO THE MUSEUM

By Trevor Andrew Bryan

"Stop day dreaming, Johanna! For the hundredth time, *please* try to *write* something."

Even more than usual, Johanna could not concentrate.

Tomorrow her class was going to visit the art museum. Johanna was so excited. She loved looking at artwork. It was one of her favorite things to do. To her, artwork was full of life and full of wonder! Johanna also couldn't wait to get as far away from this classroom as possible!

Johanna struggled in school. Whenever Mr. Sponzilli, her teacher, asked a question, Johanna tried to look as small as possible and keep her hands tucked out of sight so that Mr. Sponzilli would never call on her. But every once in a while, usually during reading, despite her best efforts to be invisible, Mr. Sponzilli would call on her. "Johanna, what do you have to say?" All the other kids would turn and stare. The result was always the same . . . red cheeks partnered with silence. Johanna couldn't read very well and never knew quite what to say. All those words and all those questions about those words didn't make any sense to her.

That night Johanna drifted off to sleep dreaming about all the wonderful paintings she would see. Johanna needed a good day.

Splash! The bus barreled through another puddle. "Can't this thing go any faster?" thought Johanna. Finally, after what seemed like forever, the bus pulled up in front of the art museum. Inside, Johanna looked around in awe. There was so much to see. She couldn't wait to start the tour. And the best part thought Johanna, "No reading!"

After the class hung up their raincoats and got their name tags in place, a man in a security uniform gave them a brief lecture. "No food. No drinks. No flash photography. Never stray from your group. And NEVER touch any of the art." Then a woman introduced herself. "Hi, I'm Ms. Brice, and I'll be your tour guide this morning. Today, when we view the artwork, we are going to think just like readers do. How does that sound?"

"Awful!" thought Johanna, "READING? REALLY?" She tucked her hands behind her back and looked at the floor.

As they approached the first painting, Johanna tried to stand in the back. However, since Johanna was little, Mrs. Sponzilli pushed Johanna to the very front.

"Okay," Ms. Brice said, "Before we start talking about the painting, let's list everything you see in the painting with the person standing next to you. Try to find about twenty things."

Johanna was next to Harry, the smartest kid in the class. Johanna stood silently as Harry started rattling off all things he saw. "A boy, a balloon, sky, legs . . ." Harry went on and on.

"How many of you were able to list about twenty things?" Ms. Brice asked. A bunch of hands shot up. Johanna held her hands behind her back. "Great!" Ms. Brice said.

"When we look at an artwork," Ms. Brice continued, "or even when you read a book, one of the best ways to start thinking about it is by thinking about the mood. So let's talk with our partners about what the mood is."

After the kids talked a moment, Ms. Brice asked, "So what's the mood of this painting?" Hands shot up. "You can all say it," said Ms. Brice. "Happy!" is what most of the kids called out. "Now, share any other words you can think of."

Joyful.

Relaxed.

Without realizing it, Johanna mumbled, "Free."

"What did you say Johanna?" asked Ms. Brice. All the eyes turned to look at Johanna. "Umm . . . Uh . . . Free." Johanna said again quietly.

"Aah, free. What a *wonderful* word to describe this picture!" Ms. Brice said. "So now let's prove it! Let's prove that *happy, joyful,* and *free* are great words to describe this painting. Let's look for the evidence."

"He's smiling!" called Vishwa.

"Yes!" said Ms. Brice. "Always look at the faces of the characters first. Brilliant!"

"His body looks like he is floating! He's not struggling."

"Very good! We can also look at character's bodies and actions to find evidence of the mood, too," Ms. Brice said. "What other evidence do we see?"

The class stood silently looking at Ms. Brice. Ms. Brice waited. Then she saw a very little hand move up just a smidge. It was Johanna's.

"What do you see that supports the mood, Johanna?"

"Colors. I see the bright colors," Johanna said quietly. "And he's floating away from the dark."

"That's right!" said Ms. Brice. "By looking at the character's face, his body, and the colors we find a pattern, kind of a pattern-ish pattern, of joy or happiness or freedom. It's up to you as the viewer to find these clues and put them together. This is also the same kind of information readers should look for. It's all the same!"

Ms. Brice patted Johanna on the shoulder. "Smart thinking!" she said.

"Now let me ask you another question. Do you think this boy is really flying? Talk to your partners about this."

The children turned and talked, sharing their thinking with each other.

"So what do you think?" Ms. Brice asked the group.

Hands shot up.

Most agreed that it wasn't meant to be a "real" image of a boy flying. As Kylie said, "One balloon, even a whole handful of balloons couldn't lift a real person, not even a kid."

"So then," Ms. Brice asked. "What does the artist want you to think about?" It was quiet. Nobody was sure what to say, not even Harry. Then a few seconds later, Johanna's hand raised, again just a bit. "What do you think, Johanna?" Ms. Brice asked.

"Umm . . . , well, maybe since this picture is about happiness and freedom, one thing that the artist might want us to think about is umm, maybe escape," Johanna said quietly.

"ESCAPE! Excellent!" Ms. Brice said. "So as a viewer and as a reader, one of your jobs is to make connections to the artworks that you are looking at or reading. Who can make a connection to the idea of escaping? What do you dream about escaping from?"

"Math!" Vishwa said.

"My younger brother!" laughed Drew.

"Bedtime!" said Kylie.

"Diabetes," said Jack.

"How about you?" Ms. Brice said looking at Johanna. "What do dream of escaping from?"

Johanna hesitated then quietly said, "I wish I could escape from not knowing how to read."

"Well you know, Johanna," said Ms. Brice. "Today you are doing the most courageous thing a viewer or reader can do. You're putting the clues together and sharing your thoughts. We are all smarter because of it. We're all smarter because of you!"

Johanna beamed.

"So another thing that viewers and readers do is think about characters and objects as symbols," Ms. Brice went on. "So in this picture, what can the yellow balloon represent? Talk to your partner."

"We came up with hope," Owen said, "because it's helping the boy escape."

"Aah, very good," said Ms. Brice. "So let's make another artwork-to-self connection. Think about what your struggle is. Do you have a symbol of hope or your own 'yellow balloon' perhaps?"

After the class discussed their "yellow balloons," they went on to look at and discuss other artworks before heading back to school. Johanna stayed close to Ms. Brice for the entire rest of the trip. On the way home, the paintings danced through Johanna's head.

The next day, Mr. Sponzilli had the class write thank-you notes to Ms. Brice. Johanna got right to her writing. She knew exactly what she wanted to write.

> Dear Ms. Brice,
> YOU are my yellow balloon. Thank you.
>
> Your friend,
> Johanna

Later during reading, Mr. Sponzilli started to read a little picture book about a girl who couldn't draw. "I thought this would be a good book after our trip to the museum," he said. After the first page, Mr. Sponzilli looked up and asked, "So what's the mood and how do we know?" Johanna's hand was the first to go up. She knew exactly what she wanted to say.

References

Barnhouse, Dorothy, and Vicki Vinton. 2012. *What Readers Really Do: Teaching the Process of Meaning Making.* Portsmouth, NH: Heinemann.

Beers, Kylene, and Robert E. Probst. 2013. *Notice and Note: Strategies for Close Reading*. Portsmouth, NH: Heinemann.

Blackburn, Laura. 2015. "Devastation in Vanuatu." With *Time* and AP. *Time for Kids*, March 16. https://www.timeforkids.com/news/devastation-vanuatu/224271.

Boushey, Gail, and Joan Moser. 2014. *The Daily 5: Fostering Literacy Independence in the Elementary Grades*. 2nd ed. Portland, ME: Stenhouse.

Boyles, Nancy. 2014. *Closer Reading, Grades 3–6: Better Prep, Smarter Lessons, Deeper Comprehension*. Thousand Oaks, CA: Corwin.

Buck, Chris, Jennifer Lee, and Shane Morris. 2013. *Frozen*. Directed by Chris Buck and Jennifer Lee. Burbank, CA: Walt Disney Studios Motion Pictures.

Burkins, Jan, and Kim Yaris. 2018. *Who's Doing the Work? Lesson Sets* Grades K–3. Portsmouth, NH: Stenhouse.

Calkins, Lucy, and Elizabeth Dunford Franco. 2015. *Building Good Reading Habits*. Units of Study for Teaching Reading: Grade 1, Unit 1. Portsmouth, NH: Heinemann.

Calkins, Lucy, and Audra Kirshbaum Robb. 2014. *Writing About Reading: From Reader's Notebooks to Companion Books*. Units of Study in Argument, Information, and Narrative Writing. Portsmouth, NH: Heinemann.

Dahl, Roald. 1982. *The BFG*. New York: Scholastic.

Davies, Jacqueline. 2007. *The Lemonade War*. Boston: Houghton Mifflin Harcourt.

DiCamillo, Kate. 2001. *The Tiger Rising*. Somerville, MA: Candlewick.

——. 2006. *Mercy Watson Goes for a Ride*. Somerville, MA: Candlewick.

Edwards-Leis, C. E. 2012. "Challenging Learning Journeys in the Classroom: Using Mental Model Theory to Inform How Pupils Think When They Are Generating Solutions." In *PATT 26 Conference: Technology Education in the 21st Century,* Stockholm, Sweden, 26–30 June, 2012, ed. Thomas Ginner, Jonas Hallström, and Magnus Hultén (pp. 153–162). Linköping, Sweden: Linköping University Electronic Press.

Ericsson, Anders, and Robert Pool. 2016. *Peak: Secrets from the New Science of Expertise*. Boston, MA: Houghton Mifflin Harcourt.

Farnsworth, Shaelynn. 2016. "What Current Brain Research Tells Us . . ." *Shaelynn Farnsworth* (blog), August 19. https://shaelynnfarnsworth.com/2016/08/19/workers-compensation-benefits.

Fletcher, Ralph. 2017. *Joy Write: Cultivating High-Impact, Low-Stakes Writing*. Portsmouth, NH: Heinemann.

Fountas, Irene, and Gay Su Pinnell. 2001. *Guiding Readers and Writers: Teaching Comprehension, Genre, and Content Literacy.* Portsmouth, NH: Heinemann.

Frankel, Erin, and Paula Heaphy. 2012. *Weird!* Minneapolis, MN: Free Spirit.

Gardiner, John Reynolds. 1980. *Stone Fox.* New York: Harper.

Gravel, Elise. 2012. *The Worm.* New York: Penguin Random House.

Harvey, Stephanie, and Anne Goudvis. 2013. "Comprehension at the Core." *Reading Teacher* 66 (6): 432–439.

Hoge, Robert. 2015. *Ugly.* New York: Scholastic.

International Literacy Association. 2018. "Why Literacy?" https://www.literacyworldwide.org/about-us/why-literacy.

Jacobs, Leland B., ed. 1965. *Using Literature with Young Children.* New York: Teachers College Press.

Kann, Victoria, and Elizabeth Kann. 2007. *Purplicious.* New York: HarperCollins.

Lehman, Chris, and Kate Roberts. 2014. *Falling in Love with Close Reading: Lessons for Analyzing Texts—and Life.* Portsmouth, NH: Heinemann.

Miller, Arthur. 1998. *Death of a Salesman.* New York: Penguin Group.

Miller, Debbie. 2002. *Reading with Meaning: Teaching Comprehension in the Primary Grades.* Portland, ME: Stenhouse.

Moser, Joan. 2017. Personal communication. July.

Parish, Peggy. 1963. *Amelia Bedelia.* New York: HarperCollins.

Paterson, Katherine. 1977. *Bridge to Terabithia.* New York: HarperCollins.

Portalupi, JoAnn, and Ralph Fletcher. 2001. *Nonfiction Craft Lessons: Teaching Information Writing K–8.* Portland, ME: Stenhouse.

Ray, Katie Wood. 2010. *In Pictures and in Words: Teaching the Qualities of Good Writing Through Illustration Study.* Portsmouth, NH: Heinemann.

Reynolds, Peter H. 2003. *The Dot*. Cambridge, MA: Candlewick.

——. 2004. *Ish*. Cambridge, MA: Candlewick.

Rosenblatt, Louise M. 1995. *Literature as Exploration*. New York: Modern Language Association of America.

Rubin, Adam, and Daniel Salmieri. 2008. *Those Darn Squirrels!* Boston: Sandpiper.

Shakespeare, William. 2011. *The Tragedy of Romeo and Juliet*, ed. Barbara A. Mowat and Paul Werstine. New York: Simon & Schuster Paperbacks.

Snicket, Lemony. 1999. A Series of Unfortunate Events. New York: HarperCollins.

Stine, R. L. 2013. *Dr. Maniac Will See You Now*. New York: Scholastic.

Taylor, Theodore. 1969. *The Cay*. New York: Yearling.

White, E. B. 1952. *Charlotte's Web*. New York: Harper.

Williams, John. 1975. *Jaws*. Universal City, CA: Universal Pictures.

Woodson, Jacqueline, and E. B. Lewis. 2001. *The Other Side*. New York: G. P. Putnam's Sons.

——. 2012. *Each Kindness*. New York: Nancy Paulsen Books.

PAINTINGS

William Merritt Chase, American, 1849–1916
Landscape: Shinnecock, Long Island, ca. 1896
Oil on wood panel
36.3 × 40.9 cm. ($14\frac{5}{16}$ × $16\frac{1}{8}$ in.)
frame: 65.1 × 69.3 × 8.5 cm ($25\frac{5}{8}$ × $27\frac{5}{16}$ × $3\frac{3}{8}$ in.)
Gift of Francis A. Comstock, Class of 1919
y1939-35

John Frederick Kensett, American, 1816–1872
Lake George, ca. 1870
Oil on academy board
36.2 × 61.9 cm. (14¼ × 24⅜ in.)
frame: 65.7 × 91.5 cm (25⅞ × 36 in.)
Bequest of Elaine King in memory of her husband, Col. Herbert G. King, Class of 1922
y1994-151